ABSTRAKT

ABSTRAKT

1999

ESSAY:
CHRISTINE BUCI-GLUCKSMANN

GALERIE THADDAEUS ROPAC
SALZBURG · PARIS

VON DER ABSTRAKTION ZU DEN ABSTRAKTEN

Seit Duchamp gibt es nur noch Ready-mades, auch wenn der Künstler das Werk eigenhändig herstellt. So die Meinung Richters über die paradoxen Herausforderungen einer abstrakten Malerei, die die von Duchamp eingeleitete und lange unterschätzte, ja ignorierte Wende, zur Kenntnis nimmt.[1] Denn das Ende der Moderne mit ihren bekannten ästhetischen Kriterien - Reinheit des Mediums, Fläche und Bild als Selbstbezug - wie auch die Krise der Postmoderne in den achtziger Jahren unseres Jahrhunderts haben dazu geführt, daß heute über zeitgenössische Abstraktionen neu nachgedacht werden muß. Mehr als bei der Abstraktion durch Elimination und Negation, die allenfalls beim Monochrom endet, sehen wir uns heute einer unreinen und komplexen Abstraktion gegenüber, die die Trennung zwischen Ausdruck und Arbeitsweise bei Malerei/Bildhauerei/Video oder dem Gegenständlichen und dem Abstrakten nicht mehr vornimmt. Also geht es um einen Folgeansatz, bei dem die von der Flächigkeit der Moderne befreite Abstraktion sich in vielen Unternehmungen, Systemen und Anlagen zeigt, die ihre eigenen Stätten und Plätze - von der Fläche über die Skulptur bis hin zur Architektur - generieren. Eine Post-Abstraktion sozusagen, mehr additiv und extraktiv als subtraktiv.[1] Sie breitet sich aus wie eine riesige Weltkarte dieser realen und virtuellen Welt, in der die allgegenwärtige Gewalt zugunsten einer kommunikativen Transparenz banalisiert wird.

Also wirkt diese Abstraktion auf den unterschiedlichen Ebenen, die Kunst und Form durchlaufen, durch Abstrakta: topologische Abstrakta aus Inflexionen, Bändern, Spiralen und Knoten (David Reed, Jonathan Lasker oder Fabian Marcaccio); Diagramme von Kreisläufen und Vernetzungen (Peter Halley, Juan Uslé oder Walter Obholzer); Abstrakta aus Rahmen und verschiedenen Monochromen (Christian Eckart, Jason Martin, Helmut Federle), landschaftsbezogene Werke (Richter, Hubert Scheibl, Imi Knoebel); biologische und kosmetische Abstrakta (Mary Heilmann, Sylvie Fleury und John Armleder). Nun ist also das Abstraktum ein plastisches Wesen und hypervisuelles Zeichen, das jede Geste und jegliche Expressivität des Bildes zugunsten einer Art abstrakter Maschine ausschaltet. Somit verweist es auf eine Geschichte der Abstraktion, die das offenkundig Heterogene kombiniert: Diagramme bei Duchamp und die skelettartigen Schemen seines Glasbildes *Die Neuvermählte wird von ihren Junggesellen entkleidet* (oder *Das große Glas*), Diagramme von Sol Lewitt oder Dan Flavin, Karten aller Art, ohne den Gegenpol zu vergessen, die dem Jugendstil eigenen Naturabstrakta oder Andy Warhols Bildbabstrakta - seriell, schematisiert und variiert. Das Abstraktum ist Code, Signatur und klares Merkmal zugleich, das sich zu einer dynamischen Bildsprache entwickelt. Aber es ist auch ein formaler Indikator, ein Artefakt, visuell so präsent, daß es mit dem Abstrakten Bildhaftigkeit schafft. Laskers *New Images*, Eckarts *Eidolon* und *Icon-Type*, der Hitchcock'sche Bilderreigen in David Reeds *Vertigo* zwischen dem "realen" Zimmer Madeleines, der Videodarstellung und dem Bild über dem Bett: hier finden wir eine potentiell abstrakte Gegenständlichkeit, einen Übergang vom Abstraktum zum Bild, ja sogar zur Skulptur, die die Bildflächen in alte, schon nicht mehr erinnerte Körper und Gesichter eintragen kann (Per Kirkeby).

Und deshalb durchqueren und vermischen diese Abstrakta die mehr oder weniger konfliktträchtigen Räume der historischen Abstraktion. Der geriffelte Raum, geometrisch und metrisch, von nun an ohne Idealismus eingesetzt: Peter Halleys urbane und soziale Karos, akzentuierte und materialisierte Bildeinstellungen bei Knoebel, Obholzer oder Eckart, horizontale Linien und winzige Raster bei Lasker. Doch dieser ideale Raum ist jetzt mit einem anderen, einem "glatten" Raum konfrontiert - einem Raum aus Wegen, Strömen und einem neuen Fließen, aus Biegungen und Krümmungen, die auf das Vergehen der Zeit hinweisen, auf ihre Vergänglichkeit und ihr Schweben. Tatsächlich besteht nämlich die Wirkung dieser Abstrakta darin (in bezug auf die traditionellen Gegensätze zwischen geometrischer und organischer Bildsprache), eine Reihe von beunruhigenden, störenden Effekten und Affekten zu erzeugen. Frei von Pathos und Lyrik, ohne Intimität, scheinen sie mir von jenem "Prinzip Gleichgültigkeit" beherrscht zu sein, das Bataille bereits bei Manet erkannte, und das schließlich von Duchamp, Warhol und Richter auf ihrer Suche nach einer "Schönheit der Gleichgültigkeit" oder der kalten, technischen Distanz beansprucht wurde, die dem Schönen gegenüber gleichgültig bleibt.

Gleichgültigkeit gegenüber der ausdrucksvollen Gestik und der malerischen Berührung zugunsten des Effekts der allgegenwärtigen Fläche. Das Bild wird durch glatte Materialien (Aluminium, polierter Stahl, Resopal oder Plexiglas), durch Lasuren, leuchtende, oft künstlich grelle Farben gewissermaßen neutralisiert, akzentuiert von technischen Lichtspielen und Formen, vervielfältigt und vervielfältigend, gefangen in ihren Spannungen und Variationen. Die Perspektive ist eine Fläche oder ein Spiegel, das Bild ein Monitor, ein Film oder eine mehr oder weniger gefaltete und verzerrte Haut. Denn die Kraft der Abstrakta wirkt nur auf der Flachheit brutal glatter, reflektierender, spiegelnder Flächen. Die Farbe verdeckt die Malerei durch ihre Glätte, ihre Lasur und ihre anonyme Objektivität: unsichtbare Schichten, unerfaßbares Fließen, äußerster Kunstgriff einer anorganischen Vitalität, fähig zur Anwendung uralter Techniken. Deshalb liegt die Wirkung der Flächen, wie bei Vermeer, im Schaffen reflexiver Bilder. Die Kunst des Malens ist eine "darstellende Kunst".

Doch scheint die Fläche selbst zwischen zwei Extremen gefangen zu sein. Sie verdeckt, glättet und schließt das Ready-made Objekt in eine rätselhafte Kontinuität ein, wie die bei Dominique Figarella in die Bildfläche inkorporierten Krawatten. Echtes oder unechtes Holz, Objekt oder nicht, die Grenze verwischt sich zugunsten einer Membran-Malerei, die das Oberflächliche und das Profunde, das Innere und das Äußere der Welt miteinander in Berührung bringt. Die Abstraktion "biegt" die Zeit, formt sie, sogar in den geologischen Schichten der Werke. Doch diese Fläche, topologisch und voller Kontaktenergie, wie man sie in den leuchtenden, rhythmischen Bewegungen der Transparenzen eines Jason Martin wiederfindet, kann sich auch öffnen. Sie schafft dann einen Raum wie im Werk Fabian Marcaccios, der über den Dimensionen zu schweben scheint. Seine großformatigen kartografischen Bilder der Welt, gefangen in den ausladenden Wellen der auf unbeweglichen Stahlstrukturen montierten Leinwand, werden allmählich zu visuellen Projektilen, zu Bilder-Skulpturen, weder stabil noch instabil. Daher ihre paradoxe Topologie: endlose Verzerrung des Auges, das Innere zum Äußeren geworden, Kontinuität und Diskontinuität, Stabilität und Fluß, Biegung und Krümmung. Man begreift, daß diese Kunst der Fläche, Schöpferin von Volumen und Bewegung, auf das architektonische Werk Greg Lynns traf, das eben das tut, nämlich den Raum aus der Fläche zu erzeugen.[3]

Doppelt belichtet oder spiegelbildlich auf sich zurückgeworfen, sich öffnend in ihre mehr oder weniger spiralförmige Bewegung, landschaftsbezogen oder leer - die Fläche ist der Sinnträger, die vierte Dimension einer Wirklichkeit, die allen Monitoren und Interfaces der Virtualität standhält. Bis zu dem Punkt, an dem die Fläche zu einem echtfalschen, gemalten Wandteppich werden kann, mit geometrischen, pastellfarbenen

Tupfern aus Schminktöpfen, die alle die feine Spur des Übergangs vom Maskulinen zum Femininen tragen, wie bei den Installationen von Sylvie Fleury und John Armleder. Doch diese erweiterte Abstraktion bleibt nicht zuletzt Gegenstand eines Experimentierens, das an Michel Foucaults *expérience du dehors* erinnert. Ohne Intimität oder Körperlichkeit extrahieren diese Abstraktionen Sichtbarkeiten der Welt, bedienen sie sich einer "gebeugten Kraft", einer Reihe von Doubles und Dubletten, einer Topologie, in der die Wirklichkeit zugleich assimiliert und ausgedrückt wird. Und es ist wohl auch diese Doppelbeziehung zwischen Fläche und Double und Fläche und dynamischer Topologie, die den Kern der Arbeiten von Richter und David Reed ausmacht. Durch all ihre Ähnlichkeiten und Unterschiede hindurch erkennen wir den Umfang und die Transformationen einer sich zur Fläche wandelnden Malerei.

Bilder von Türen und von Vorhängen, Städte, von oben betrachtet, graue Monochrome, die das Nichts und die Gleichgültigkeit visualisieren, Gläser, gemalte Spiegel, Stilleben mit zwei Kerzen, Wolken und Verkündigungen - überall "fixiert" das Spiel der einen, lasierten Fläche die Affekte durch eine neutrale und kalte Distanz, die Richter immer wieder erforscht. Diese Kunst des Doubles ist keinesfalls ein Täuschungsmanöver oder eine Simulation. Sie nimmt eher eine Art Doppelfang des Sichtbaren und Unsichtbaren vor, in einer ambiguosen Transparenz, die den Blick klärt. Somit ist die abstrakte Vorgehensweise etwas, das der Malerei innewohnt, wobei die Abspaltung der nach Fotos und Vorlagen gemalten Bilder von den "abstrakten" Werken herbeigeführt wird. Denn auch wenn ein Foto ein "reines" Bild ist, banal und ohne Stil, verfügt es dennoch über seine "eigene Abstraktion".[4] Umgekehrt verweisen abstrakte Werke auf das, was man als "Proto-Bild" bezeichnen könnte, oft landschaftsbezogen und kosmisch, stets Matrix der Abstraktion. Mit ihren visualisierten Regenschauern und Vorhängen, ihren häufigen Fragementerweiterungen und in ihrer reflektierenden Art, halten die "abstrakten" Bilder die Welt wie ein fließender, schwebender Spiegel fest, und die Zeit wird zur Form selbst des Raums. Solche Proto-Bilder, in der Abstraktion und durch sie verborgen, finden sich bei Imi Knoebel wie auch bei Juan Uslé oder Hubert Scheibl. Hier unterstreichen und umschließen Fensterrahmen das leichte und schwebende Blau des Meeres. Dort führt das Eindringen in den illusionistischen Raum der Proto-Bilder mit ihren Abweichungen und ihrer virtuellen Vielfalt zu einer Erfahrung von Dauerhaftigkeit, wobei die Leinwand, einem flüchtigen Bild gleich, sich zwischen Starrheit und Bewegung wendet. Denn die Proto-Bilder, die der abstrakten Energie der Fläche innewohnen, schaffen dank einer veritablen Kartografie der "Übergänge" und landschaftsbezogenen Reflexionen, die Licht und Linien immanent sind, und deren sich Hubert Scheibl bedient, alle möglichen Formen von Interaktionen. Doch die Fläche kann sich auch verdichten und der Radikalität des Schwarz weichen, mit allen Streifen und Riffeln der unendlich vielen räumlichen Schichtungen, wie sie den Bildern Günter Umbergs eigen sind. Eine schwarze Epiphanie, wo die Bildfläche plötzlich eine Tiefe gewinnt, die die Wand durchbohrt.

Zweifellos würde man diese Fantasmagorie der Fläche und glatten Haut der Welt im Werk David Reeds wiederfinden. Doch der Spiegel ist zu einem riesigen Monitor geworden, auf dem die Bänder - jene Blumenartefakte einer künstlichen und nicht organischen Abstraktion - sich falten, wieder auseinanderfalten, sich drehen und wenden. Das Proto-Bild ist in einer opakten Transparenz völlig verschwunden. Also ist es das dem Abstraktum immanente Fließen, das sich als potentielles Bild und Scheinfotografie reflektiert und die eigene Virtualität erzeugt. Wie im historischen Materialismus wird die Neutralisierung des Ausdrucks nicht durch Grautöne, sondern durch lebendige, kräftige, post-warholsche Farben erreicht. Auch die gebogenen und geknoteten Formen - aus Inflexionen und einer Stärke heraus, die an die Mathematik und die barocke Malerei gemahnen - durchdringen buchstäblich den Raum ihrer eigenen Macht. Als ob die Begegnung von Fließendem und virtueller Dynamik das Bild seiner Fläche und seiner Wand entreißen und damit eine ambiguose Räumlichkeit, ja einen Schock erzeugen würde. So daß die Bilder bereits "Fragmente implizierter Installationen" wären, wie Arthur Danto anmerkt. Denn hier ist die Abstraktion auf direkte Weise topologisch, und die Formen der Falten mit ihren seltsamen Punkten, ihren unerklärlichen Überlappungen, ihren ungeheuren, unendlichen, panoramischen Räumen, eingekeilt, aufeinandergetürmt, vermischt und oft gespalten, heben das Werk auf seine eigene Morphogenese. Mit seinen schlangengleichen Figuren und Riesenformaten läuft es ab wie ein Film. Als ob David Reed auf den glatten, reflektierenden Grund des Monitors unterschiedliche und hermaphroditische Streifen projizieren würde, die einen in völlig künstlichen Voluten, die andern wie kaum angelegte Schleier, wahre Spuren multiplen Schaffens. Denn jede Falte, jedes dargestellte "Band" ist doppelt zu sehen. Das Innere ist außen, und hinter diesem Schirm aus überlagerten Bildschichten gibt es nichts - wie bei den blanken, asymmetrischen Leerstellen bei bestimmten Bildenr, die die Wüste in ihrer Weite heraufbeschwören. Vorn jedoch, und wie auf dem Monitor, gewinnt die Abstraktion figürliche Kraft und ruft ein ganzes Netz von Assoziationen und heterogenen Bildern hervor: Blumen, barocke Faltenwürfe, ornamentale Muster; oder Körper, eingerollt an irgendeinem unbekannten, intimen Ort, wo Sehen Berühren heißt... "'I want to be a bedroom painter", meinte David Reed nicht ohne Humor.[5]

Zwischen Fläche und Abstraktum, Spiegel und Monitor, Europa und USA, in ihren Falten, dem Wieder-Zusammen- und Auseinanderfalten erzählen uns die Abstraktions-Abstrakta von der Welt. Einer Welt, wo man von der Kultur des Objekts auf die des Fließenden übergeht, und wo Affekte künftig an ihrer Wirkung gemessen werden. Dies wäre also ein möglicher Status der Abstraktion im "virtuellen Zeitalter", um mit Walter Benjamin zu sprechen. Ein historisches Zeitalter, in dem die alten Grenzen der Künste durch die Herrschaft der Bilder und der Mannigfaltigkeit aufgehoben werden. Hier wird die Malerei zur Skulptur, zur Monitor-Leinwand und zum Interface und das Abstraktum zu der Kunst, Fläche zu besetzen, sie zu strukturieren und die universalen Linien und Effekte komplexer Bilder zu erzeugen. Denn es geht eher darum, Beziehungen, Spannungen und Kräfte darzustellen als Objekte und Modelle. Das Abstraktum ist somit ein Multiplikator heterogener Räume, in denen die Zeit logiert. Ein fließendes Dauern, flüchtige und vergängliche Augenblicke, plötzlich mit einer künstlichen und technologischen Welt konfrontiert, die die Malerei durch jene seltsame "Anästhesie" der Netzhaut auf Distanz hält, die Duchamp auf seiner Suche nach der hauchdünnsten Fläche reklamierte. Denn "das Mögliche ist eine Hauchdünne" - des Irisierenden, Perlmuttschimmernden, des Transparenten und aller Reflexionen in Spiegel und Glas.

Christine Buci-Glucksmann

[1] Vgl. Richter, *Ausgewählte Texte* (Les Presses du réel), S. 115.
[2] Zu dieser Frage der Abstraktion verweise ich auf den Katalog *Nuevas Abstracciones*, Museu National Reina Sofia, Madrid und Museu d'Art contemporani, Barcelona. Ich befasse mich hier mit den Themen, die in "Vers une post abstraction" (Rue Descartes, No. 16, *Pratiques abstraites*, avril 1997, franko-amerikanisches Kolloquium, organisiert von Catherine Perret, Galerie Thaddaeus Ropac, Paris) und in meinem auf französisch und deutsch erschienen Buch *Der kartographische Blick der Kunst*, Merve Verlag, Berlin 1998, abgehandelt werden.
[3] Über diese Zusammenarbeit zwischen Malerei und Architektur vgl. die kürzlich in Wien eröffnete Ausstellung.
[4] Richter, a.a.O., S. 77
Ich hatte die Gelegenheit, diese Themen kürzlich während eines Kolloquiums anläßlich der Richter-Ausstellung auf der MACBA in Barcelona zu diskutieren. (Wird publiziert).
[5] Arthur C. Danto, "Bedside Manner", *Artforum*, Sommer 1999, und Katalog David Reed, Cantz.
[6] Duchamp, *Notes*, Champs Flammarion, S. 21 ff.

FROM ABSTRACTION TO ABSTRACTS

"Since Duchamp, we have all been making readymades, even when we paint them by hand." This was how Gerhard Richter expressed the paradoxical challenge facing a practice of abstract painting that had integrated the implications of Duchamp's revolution, in a field where this had long been underestimated, or even ignored.[1] The end of modernism and the reign of its well-known aesthetic criteria (the purity of the medium, the planar, self-referential nature of the painting), followed by the crisis of 1980s pictorial postmodernism, means that we need to rethink contemporary forms of abstraction in new terms. Instead of abstraction by elimination and negation, culminating in the pure limit of the monochrome, what we now have before us is an impure, complex abstraction which rides roughshod over the barriers that separate the practices and languages of painting from those of sculpture and of video, and divide the figurative from the abstract. This is a kind of meta-abstraction, one freed from the modernist plane and ready to engage in all kinds of operations and systems that engender their own places, moving from surface to sculpture and even to architecture. This post-abstraction, as we might call it, is more additive and extractive than subtractive.[2] It is like a great mapping of the world, of the real and the virtual worlds, in which ubiquitous violence is ideologically banalised in favour of communicational transparency.

Thus, through the different arts and forms, this abstraction functions in terms of *abstracts;* the topological abstracts of inflections, ribbons, spirals and knots (David Reed, Jonathan Lasker and Fabian Marcaccio), diagrammatic abstracts of circuits and networks (Peter Halley, Juan Uslé and Walter Obholzer), landscape abstracts (Richter, Hubert Scheibl, Imi Knoebel) or biological and cosmetic abstracts (Mary Heilmann, Sylvie Fleury and John Armleder). The abstract is a plastic entity and a hypervisual sign that distances any form of pictorial gesture or expressivity in favour of a kind of abstract machine. This is why the history of abstraction on which it is predicated is full of flagrantly heterogeneous elements – the skeletal schemas of the *Large Glass* and diagrams by Duchamp (again), Sol LeWitt and Dan Flavin, all manner of maps or, at the other extremity, the abstracts of nature characteristic of Art Nouveau and Warhol's abstracts of images, obtained by serialisation, schematisation or variation. The abstract is at once a code, a signature and a distinctive sign. It takes shape within a dynamic pictorial syntax. But it is also a formal index, an artefact that is so present visually that it creates images out of abstraction. In Lasker's "new images", Eckart's *Eidolon* and *Icon-Type*, or the Hitchcockian circuit of images in David Reed's *Vertigo* (between Madeleine's "real" room, her video image and the painting above the bed) we have a potentially figurative abstraction, a transition from abstract to image, and even to sculpture, which may inscribe its pictorial planes within bodies and faces of more ancient origin (Per Kirkeby).

Hence, these abstracts go back over and mix the more or less conflictual spaces of historical abstraction, using its striated, geometrical and metrical space without idealism. Witness Peter Halley's urban and social grids, the emphatic and fully materialised framings of Knoebel, Obholzer and Eckart, Lasker's horizons and mini-grids.

But this ideal space is now confronted with another "smooth" space constituted by trajectories, fluxes, new fluidities and curves, which indicate the passing of time, its fugacity or suspension. For the impact of these abstracts is such that it engenders a series of disruptive effects and affects in relation to the traditional opposition between geometric and organic languages. Devoid of pathos and lyricism, and quite without intimacy, they are, it seems to me, governed by "the "principle of indifference" that Bataille" saw at work in Manet, and that was later taken up by Duchamp, Warhol and Richter in their search for the "beauty of indifference", for a cold and mechanical distance that is indifferent to beauty.

These abstracts are indifferent, first of all, to expressive gesture and pictorial touch, which are jettisoned in favour of an omnipresent surface effect. The painting is "neutralised" by smooth materials (aluminium, polished steel, formica or plexiglass), by glazes, by bright, raw and often artificial colours which are emphasised by the play of hi-tech lighting and machine-made, duplicated and duplicating forms that are exploited for their variations and tensions. The quality of vision is that of a surface or a mirror; the picture object is a screen, a film or skin that may be more or less folded and deformed. For the power of these abstracts is effective only against the flatness of violently planar, reflective and mirror-like surfaces. By its smoothness, glaze and anonymous objectivity, the paint conceals the painting: in these invisible layerings and indiscernible flows lies the extreme artifice of an inorganic vitality ready to exploit the most venerable techniques. That is why, as in Vermeer, the surface effects create reflective/reflexive paintings. Pictorial art is an "art of depiction." But the surface itself seems to be caught between two extremes. Planar, it dissimulates, flattens and encloses the "readymade" object within an enigmatic continuity, like the neckties incorporated into the pictorial plane by Dominique Figarella. Real or fake wood, object or non-object-limits disappear, giving way to a membranous painting that brings together the superficial and the profound, the interior and the exterior of the world. Abstraction "folds" and modulates time in the geological strata of the pictorial. But this topological, energy-charged surface, such as we find it in the luminous and rhythmic movements of Jason Martin's transparencies, can also be unfolded. It then engenders space, as in the work of Fabian Marcaccio, which seems to skim over the dimensions. In the enveloping undulation of canvases mounted on rigid steel structures, his vast cartographic paintings of the world are gradually transformed into visual projectiles, in painting/sculptures that are neither stable nor unstable. Hence their paradoxical topology: an infinite twisting of the gaze, interior as exterior, continuity and discontinuity, stability and fluidity, fold and re-fold. One can see how this art of surfaces which creates volumes and movements should come into relation with the architectural work of Greg Lynn, in which space is generated from surface.[3]

Superimposed and folded in on itself like a mirror, unfolded in degrees of spiralling movement, landscape or void – the surface is the place of meaning, the fourth dimension of a real assayed by all the screens and interfaces of the virtual. In the work of Sylvie Fleury and John Armleder, the surface thus becomes a false mural "carpet" of paint, complete with geometrical pastel dots from the world of cosmetics, all marked by the subtle movement from masculine to feminine. But this broadened abstraction remains the object of an experiment close to what Michel Foucault called an "experience of the outside". Without intimacy or flesh, these abstractions extract visibilities from the world and practise a "folded force" through a whole series of doubles and duplications, a topology in which the real is both assimilated and exteriorised. For it is indeed this dual relation between surface and lining, surface and dynamic topology, that we find at the centre of the work by Richter and David Reed. Their similarities and differences enable us to gauge the range of transformations undergone by painting-as-surface.

Paintings of doors, of curtains, of cities seen from above, grey monochromes visualising nothingness and indifference, glass, painted mirrors, Vanitas with two candles, clouds and annunciations – everywhere, the pure glazed surface "freezes affect" in the cold, neutral distance that Richter has explored unceasingly. But this art of the double is in no sense a simulacrum or a simulation. It results, rather, from a dual capture of the visible and the invisible in an ambiguous transparency that purifies the gaze. Thus the abstract operation is internal to the paintings. It lies in the overlapping that occurs between the paintings from photographs and images and the "abstract" paintings. For if a photograph is a "pure image", banal and without style, it still has "its own form of abstraction".[4] Conversely, the abstract canvases point to what we might call a proto-image, often cosmic or landscape-based, and always a generator of abstraction. Thus, with their visual "rain" and "curtains", their repetitive enlargement of fragments and their reflectivity, the "abstract" paintings capture the world in the manner of a fluid, floating mirror in which time itself becomes the form of space. These proto-images, hidden in and by abstraction, can also be found in Imi Knoebel, as well as in Juan Uslé and Hubert Scheibl. Here emphatic frames-cum-windows enclose a floating, light marine blue. There, penetration of the space of illusions, of proto images, with their off-centredness and virtual multiplicity, gives rise to an experience of duration in which the canvas metamorphoses into the equivalent of a fleeting image, between fixity and motion. For these proto-images found within the abstract energy of the surface create all kinds of interactions, mapping "passages" and the reflections of landscape that are immanent in light and line (see the work of Hubert Scheibl). But the surface can also grow opaque and give way to the radicality of black, with the striations and stripes of layer upon spatial layer in the paintings of Günter Umberg: a black epiphany in which the visual plane suddenly takes on an intense, wall-piercing depth.

No doubt we could find this same fantasy of the surface and of the smoothed skin of the world in the work of David Reed. But here the mirror has become a giant screen where ribbons-artefacts-cum-flowers of an artificial, non-organic abstraction-fold, unfold, twist and turn. The proto-image has disappeared in an opaque transparency. Here it is the fluidity immanent within the abstract that is reflected in a potential image, in a false photograph that engenders its own virtuality. As in Renaissance Mannerism, the neutralisation of expression is achieved not by grey but by bright, post-Warholian colours that are always very physical. Thus curved and knotted forms produced by inflections and forces close to those of mathematics and Baroque painting literally traverse the space with their power. It is as if the coming together of fluidity and virtual dynamics wrested the painting from its plane and its wall by creating an ambiguous spatiality, a kind of shock effect, so that these paintings are, as Arthur Danto has observed, already "fragments of implicit installations". For here the abstraction is directly topological, and the forms of the folds with their nodal points, their unfindable coverings-over, their huge and infinite, interlocking, superimposed and mixed and often doubled-over panoramic spaces, raise painting to the level of its own morphogenesis. In these serpentine figures and huge formats, painting is played out like a film. It is as if Reed is "projecting" his differential and hermaphroditic strips onto the smooth, reflective ground of his screen.

Some are totally artificial volutes, others like veils just placed there, like traces of multiple pictorial operations. For every fold, every pictorial "ribbon" is duplicitous. The interior is the exterior and behind the screen of these superimposed pictorial strata there is nothing (the white, asymmetrical voids in certain paintings are like expanses of desert). But in front of the screen, and somehow across it, abstraction becomes a figural power evoking a whole web of heterogeneous associations and images: flowers, Baroque drapery, ornamental motifs or bodies nestling in some unknown, intimate place where seeing is touching. "I want to be a bedroom painter" is Reed's wry comment.[5]

And so, between surface and abstract, mirror and screen, Europe and USA, in their folds, re-folds and unfoldings, these abstractions/abstracts speak to us of the world. A world where we are moving from a culture of objects to a culture of flows, and where affect is now measured by effect. Such is one possible status for abstraction in what Walter Benjamin might have dubbed "the age of the virtual", a historic moment when the frontiers of art are being redrawn by the reign of images and multiplicities. Here, painting becomes sculpture, the canvas a screen and interface, and the abstract an art of inhabiting and ordering surfaces, of engendering line-worlds and complex image effects. Painting here depicts relations, tensions and forces, not objects or models. Here, the abstract becomes a multiplier of heterogeneous spaces where time is lodged. A fluid duration, fugitive and ephemeral moments suddenly faced with an artificial and technological world that painting keeps at a distance by resorting to that curious retinal "anaesthesia" advocated by Duchamp in his quest for the infra-thinness of surfaces. For "possibility is infra-thin", like iridescence, the nacreous, transparency and all reflections in mirrors and glass.[6]

Christine Buci-Glucksmann

[1] Gerhard Richter, translated from *Textes,* (Les Presses du réel), p. 115.

[2] On this question, see the catalogue *Nuevas Abstracciones* (Museo National Reina Sofia, Madrid, and Museu d'Art Contemporani, Barcelona). The themes considered in this text are also discussed in "Vers une post-abstraction" (Rue Descartes, No. 16, "Pratiques abstraites", April 1997. Proceedings from a Franco-American symposium organised by Catherine Perret/Galerie Thaddaeus Ropac, Paris), and in my book *Der kartographische Blick der Kunst,* (Merve Verlag, Berlin, 1998).

[3] For this relation between painting and architecture, see the exhibition that has just opened in Vienna.

[4] Gerhard Richter, *op. cit.,* p. 77.
I also explored these themes at a talk given recently during the Richter show at the MACBA, Barcelona (publication forthcoming).

[5] Cf. Arthur Danto, "Bedside Manner", *Artforum,* Summer 1999, and the catalogue *David Reed* (Cantz Verlag).

[6] Translated from Marcel Duchamp, *Notes* (Champs Flammarion), p. 21 ff.

ABBILDUNGEN / PLATES

JOHN ARMELDER/SYLVIE FLEURY

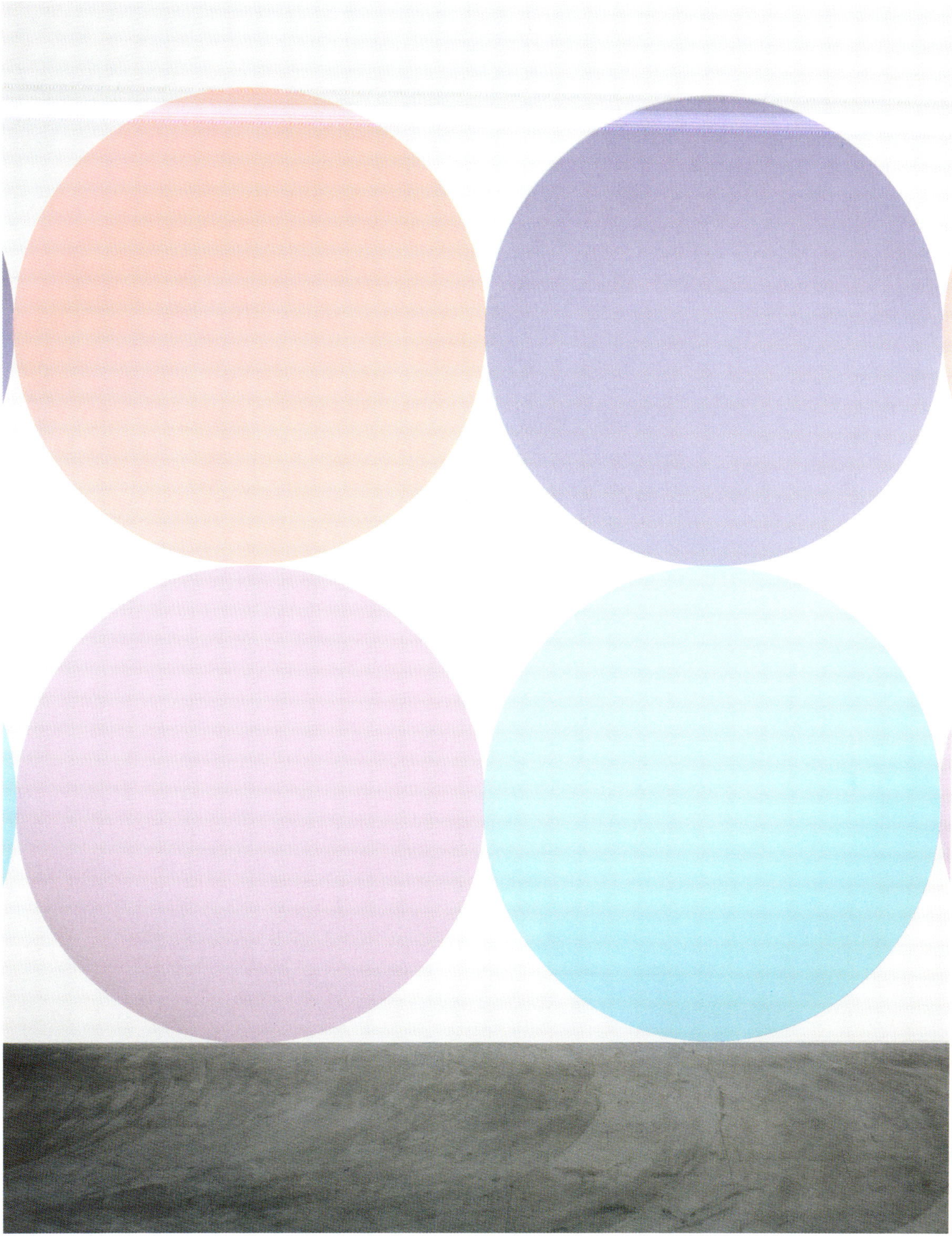

"CAMOUFLAGE I"
1998/99
ACRYL AUF WAND / WALL PAINTING, ACRYLIC
INSTALLATIONSAUFNAHME / INSTALLATION VIEW

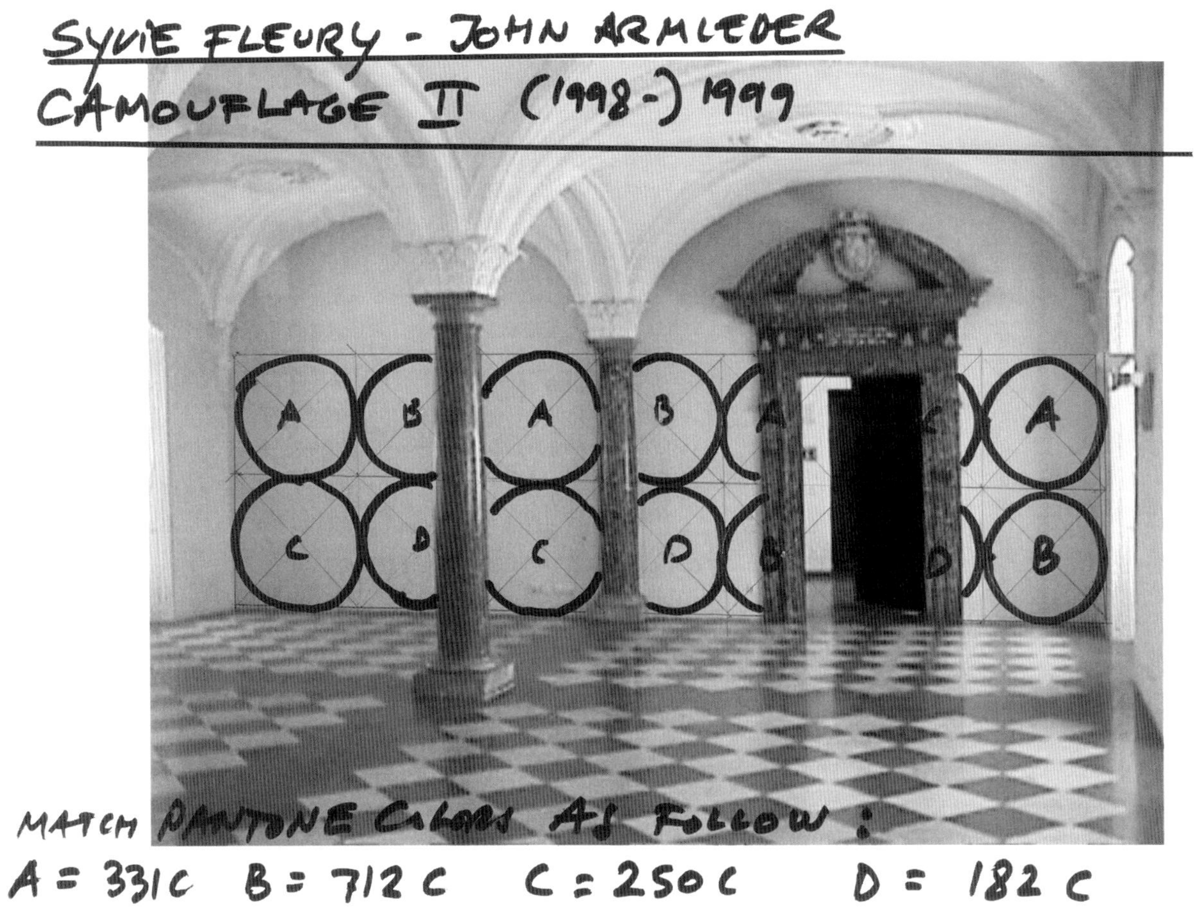

"CAMOUFLAGE II"
1999
ENTWURFSZEICHNUNG
SKETCH

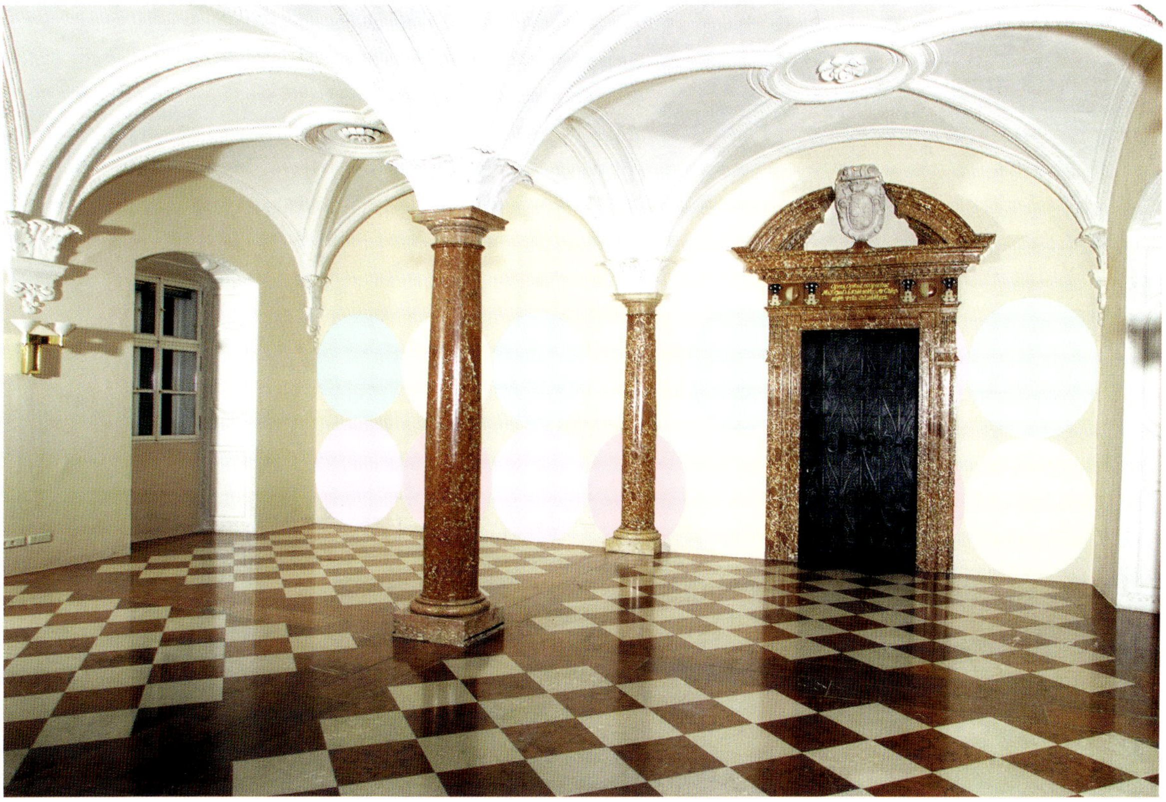

"CAMOUFLAGE II"
1999
ACRYL AUF WAND / WALL PAINTING, ACRYLIC
INSTALLATIONSAUFNAHME / INSTALLATION VIEW

CHRISTIAN ECKART

"EIDOLON #1104"

1989

BLATTGOLD AUF HOLZ · 245 X 153,5 CM

GOLD LEAF ON WOOD · 96,5 X 60,4 IN.

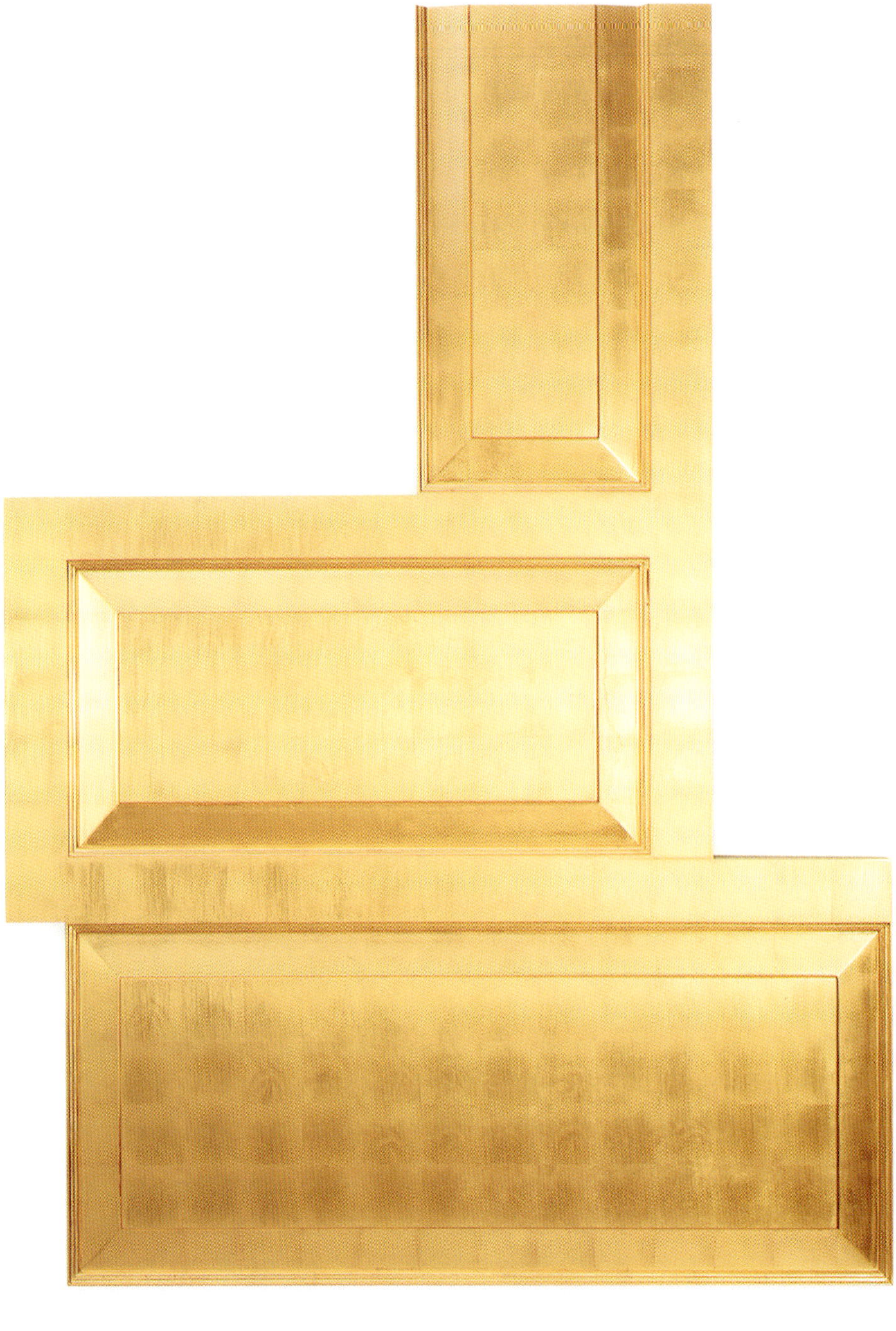

"ICON-TYPE, FRAGMENT #911"
1998
LACK UND BLATTGOLD AUF HOLZ · 160 X 114,3 CM
VARNISH AND GOLD LEAF ON WOOD · 63 X 45 IN.

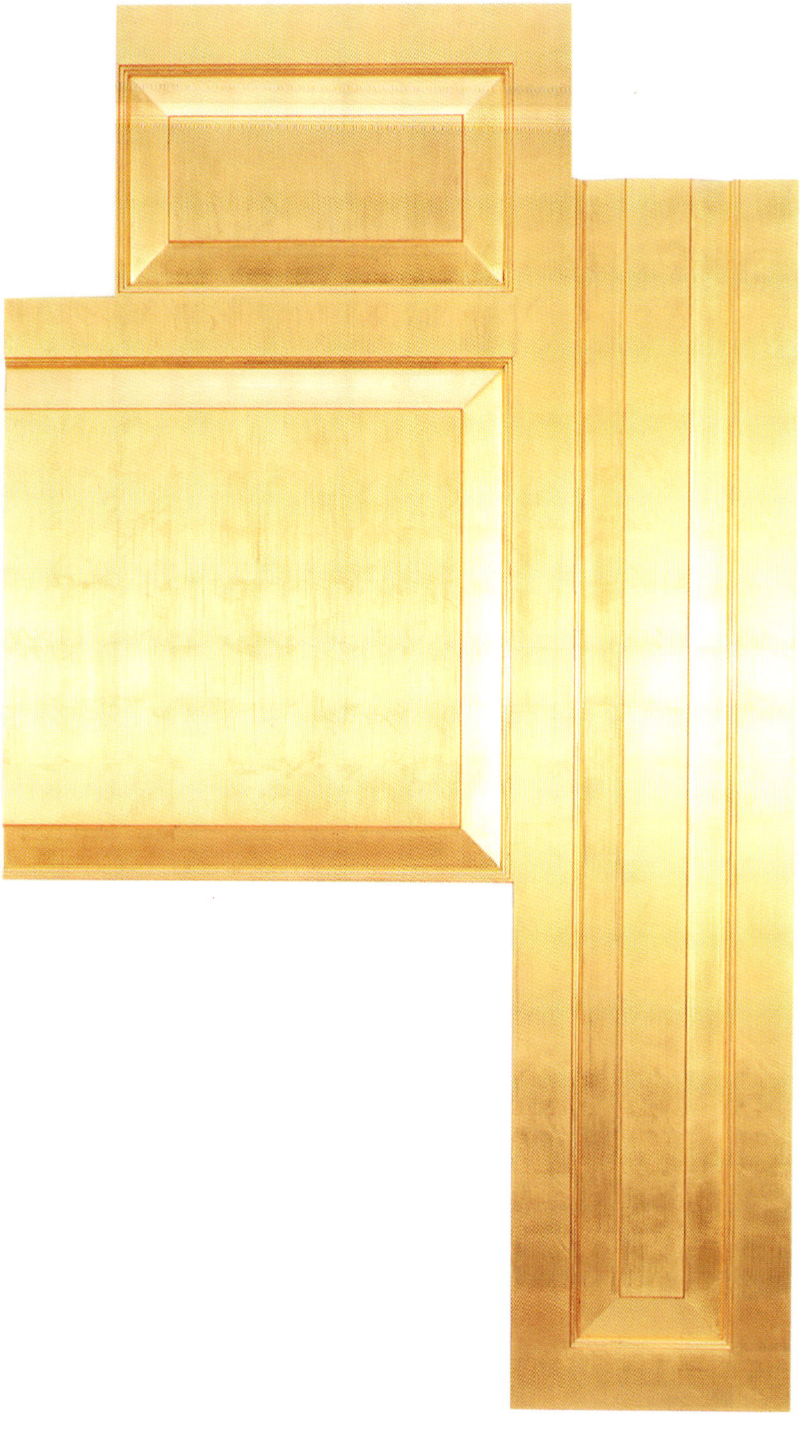

"ICON-TYPE, FRAGMENT #913"

1998

LACK UND BLATTGOLD AUF HOLZ · 183 X 106,7 CM

VARNISH AND GOLD LEAF ON WOOD · 72 X 42 IN.

HELMUT FEDERLE

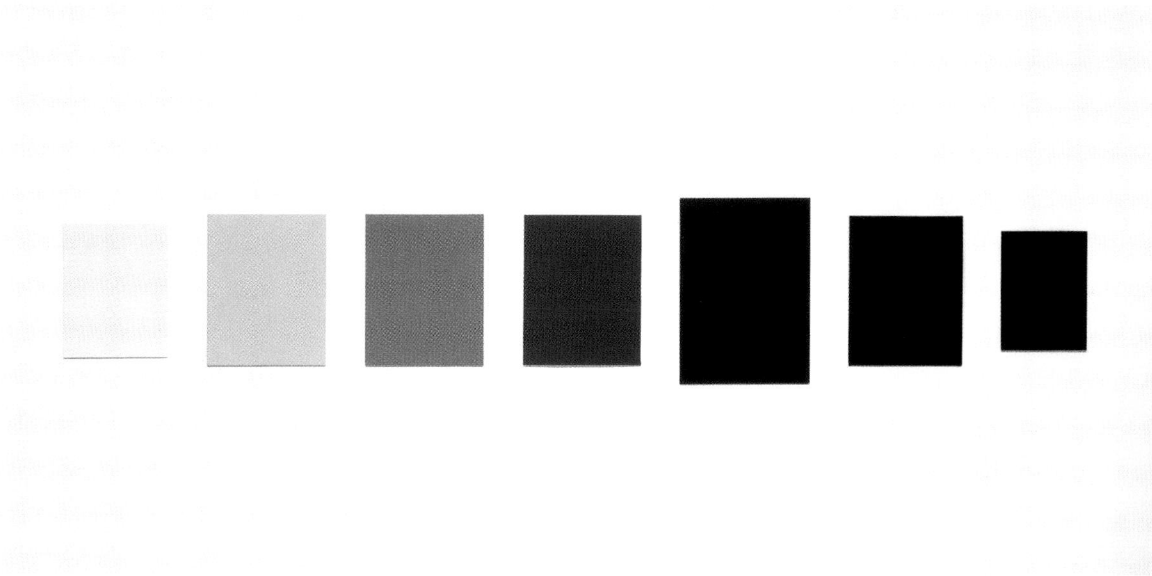

"BLACK SERIES XII"

1996

ÖL AUF LEINENKARTON · SIEBENTEILIG, GESAMT 37 X 210 CM

OIL ON HARDENED CANVAS IN SEVEN SECTIONS · 14,6 X 82,7 IN.

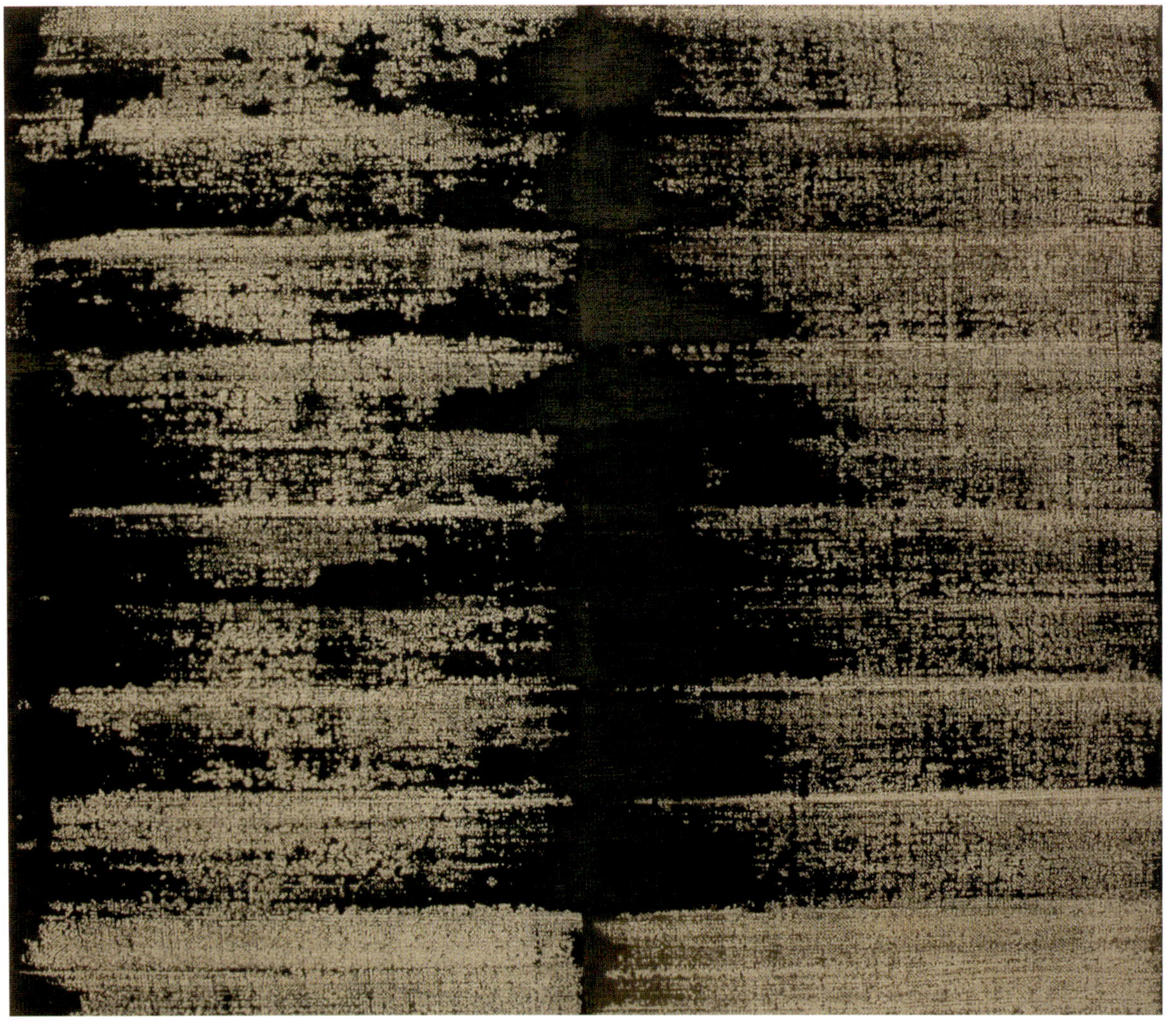

"LEGION XXV"
1999
ACRYL UND ÖL AUF LEINWAND · 50 X 58 CM
ACRYLIC AND OIL ON CANVAS · 19,7 X 22,8 IN.

"LEGION XXVIII (TWO SIDE PAINTING)"

1999

ACRYL AUF LEINWAND · 50 X 60 CM

ACRYLIC ON CANVAS · 19,7 X 23,6 IN.

DOMINIQUE FIGARELLA

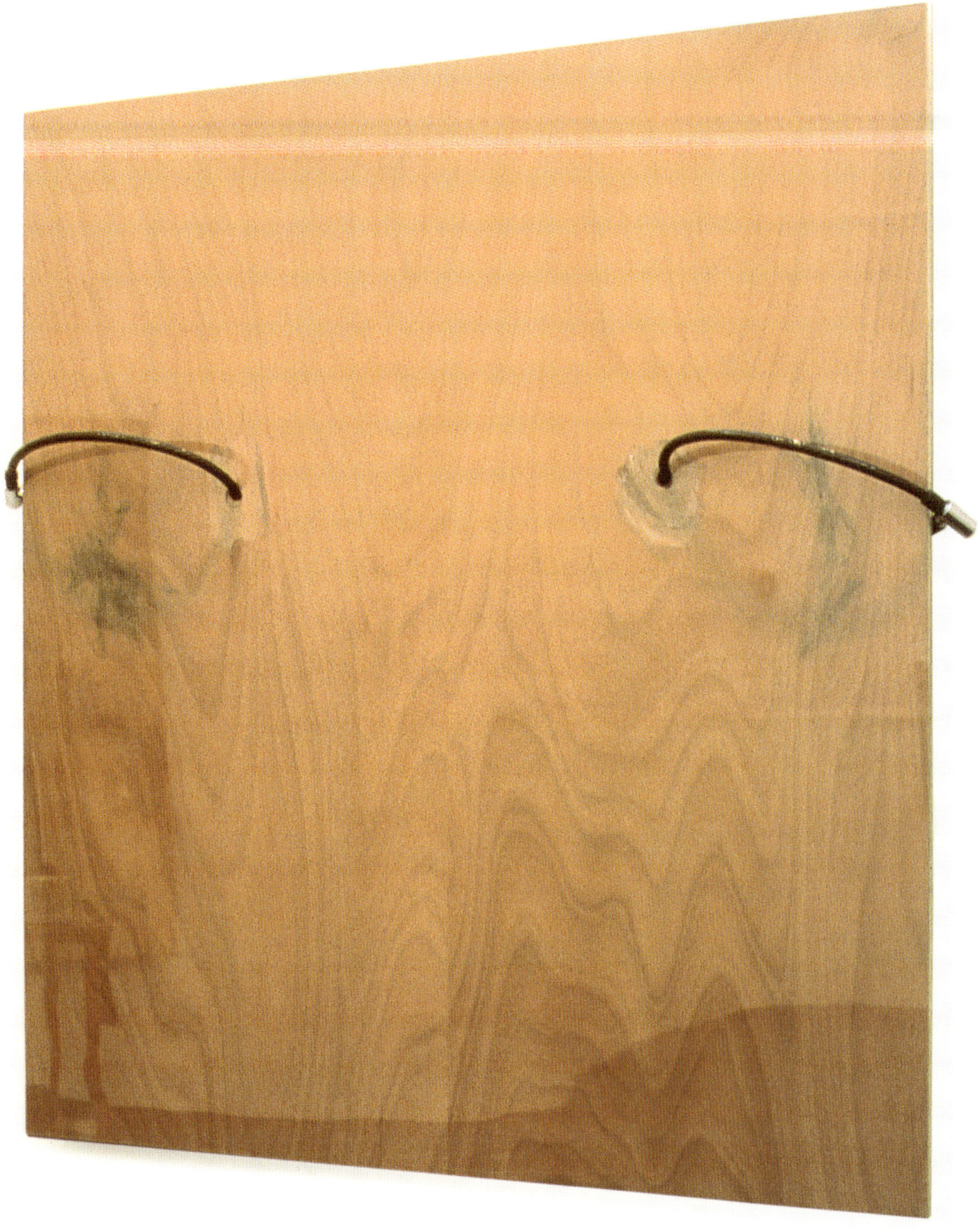

OHNE TITEL / UNTITLED

1999

LEXAN, BULLTEX, CELLOPHAN, ACRYL UND ÖL AUF HOLZ · 156 X 156 X 15 CM

LEXAN, BULLTEX, CELLOPHANE, ACRYLIC AND OIL ON WOOD · 61,4 X 61,4 X 5,9 IN.

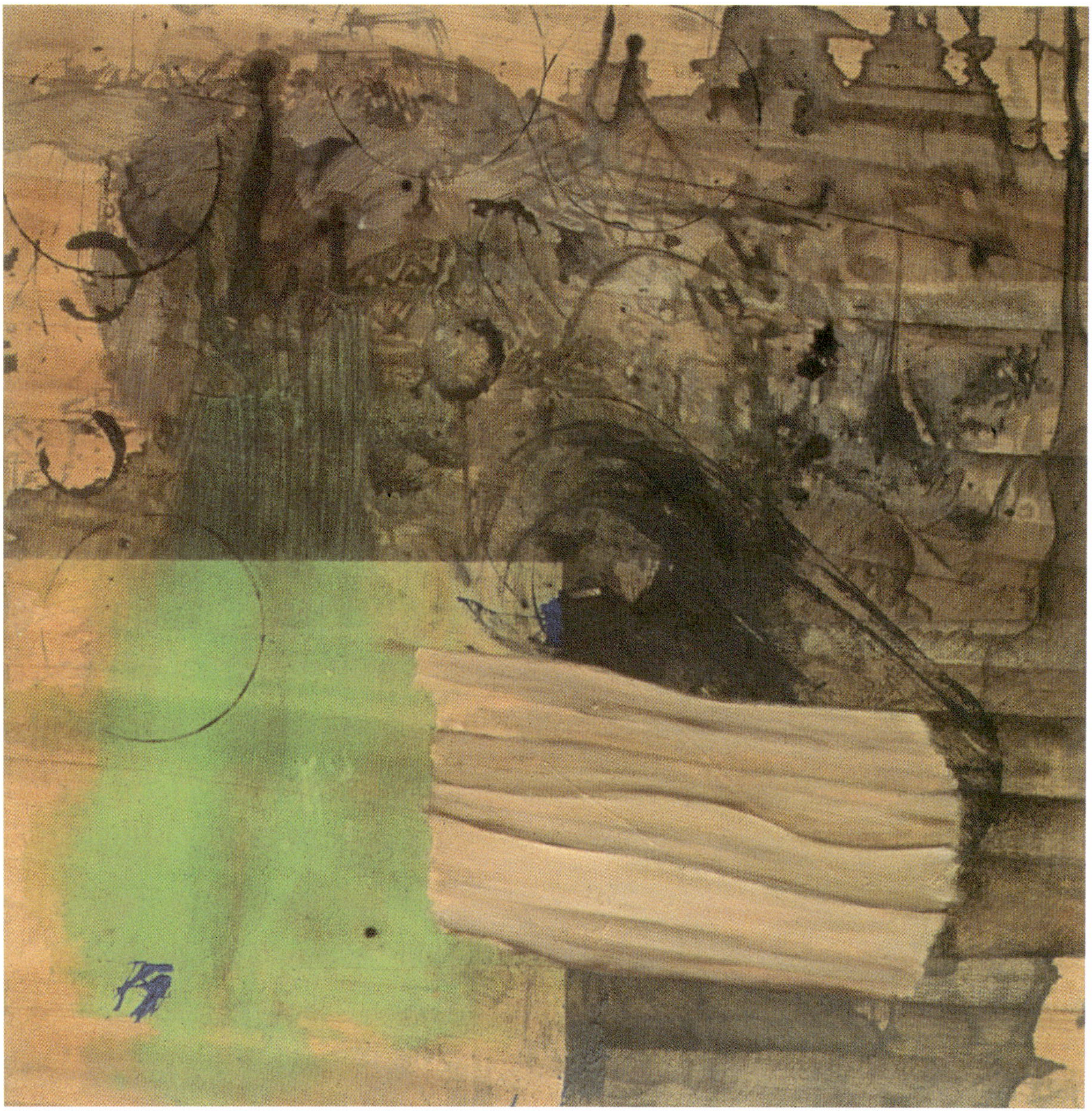

OHNE TITEL / UNTITLED

1998

BLEISTIFT, ÖL AUF HOLZ · 100 X 100 X 3 CM

GREY PENCIL, OIL ON WOOD · 39,4 X 39,4 X 1,2 IN.

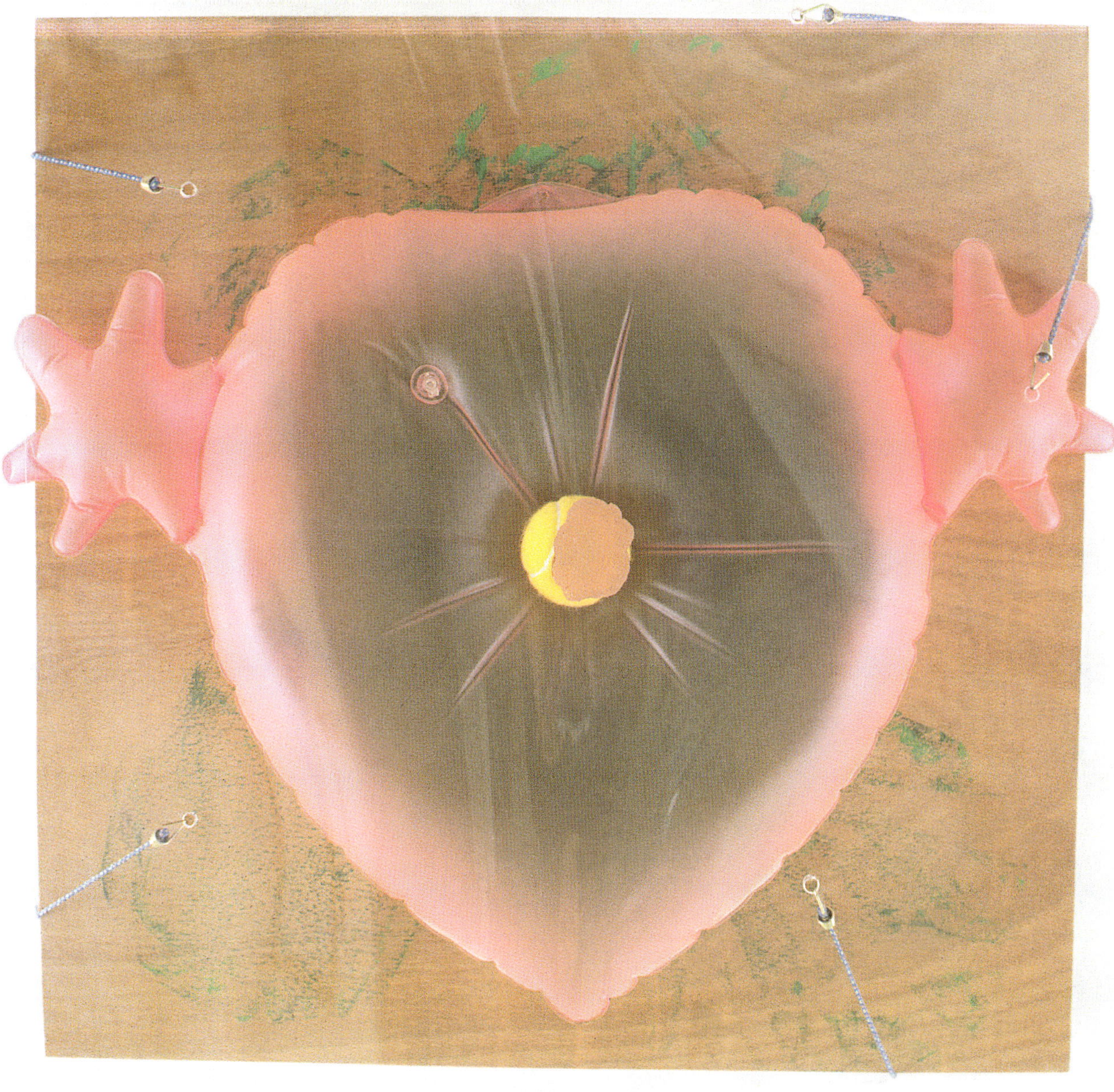

OHNE TITEL / UNTITLED

1997

TENNISBALL, SPANNER, LEXAN, BALL UND ACRYL AUF HOLZ · 70 X 70 X 20 CM

TENNIS BALL, STRETCHERS, LEXAN, BALL AND ACRYLIC ON WOOD · 27,6 X 27,6 X 7,9 IN.

PETER HALLEY

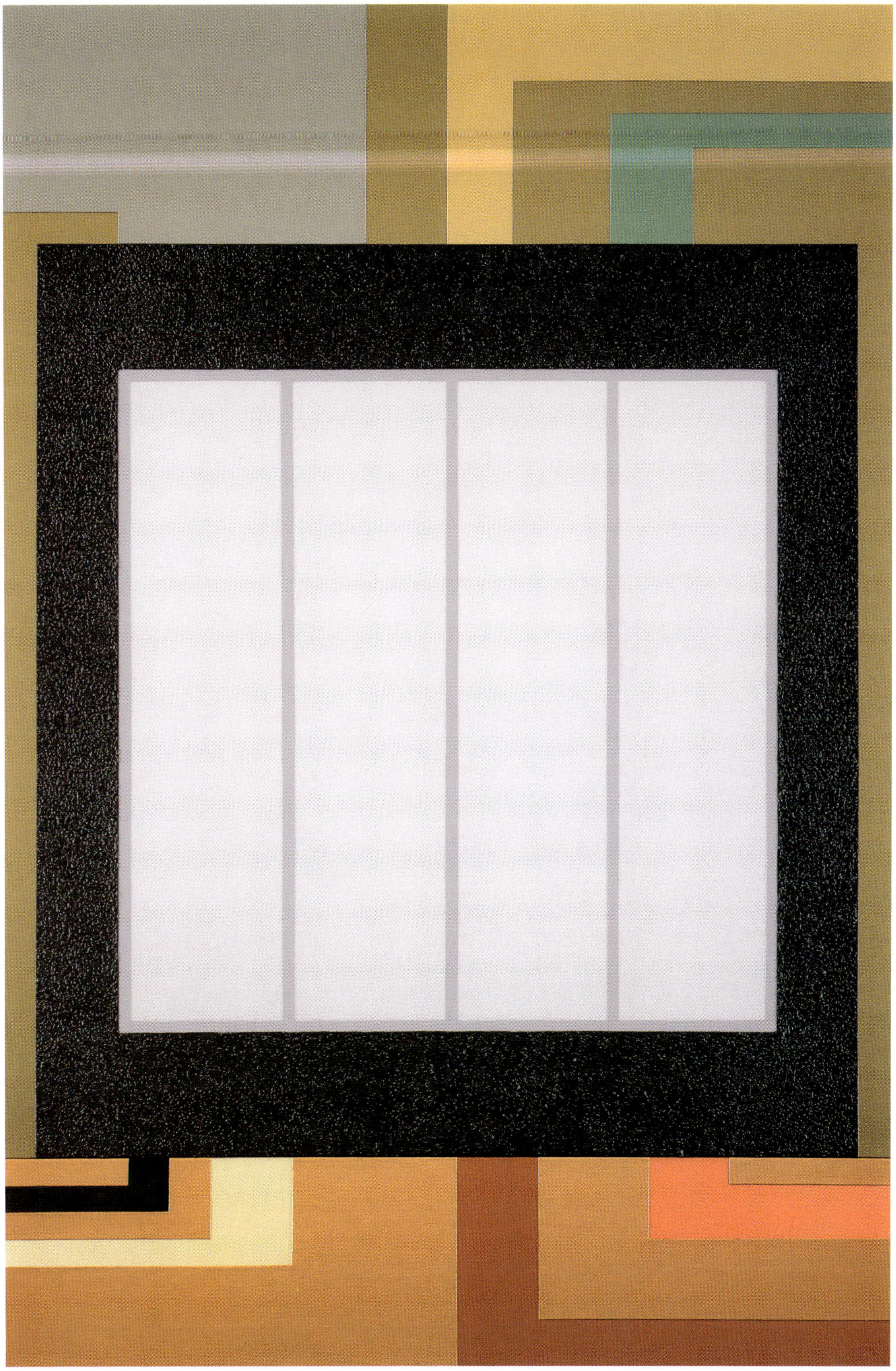

OHNE TITEL / UNTITLED

1999

ACRYL, METALLISCH GLÄNZENDES ACRYL UND ROLL-A-TEX AUF LEINWAND · 229 X 155 CM

ACRYLIC, METALLIC AND PEARLESCENT ACRYLIC AND ROLL-A-TEX ON CANVAS · 90 X 61 IN.

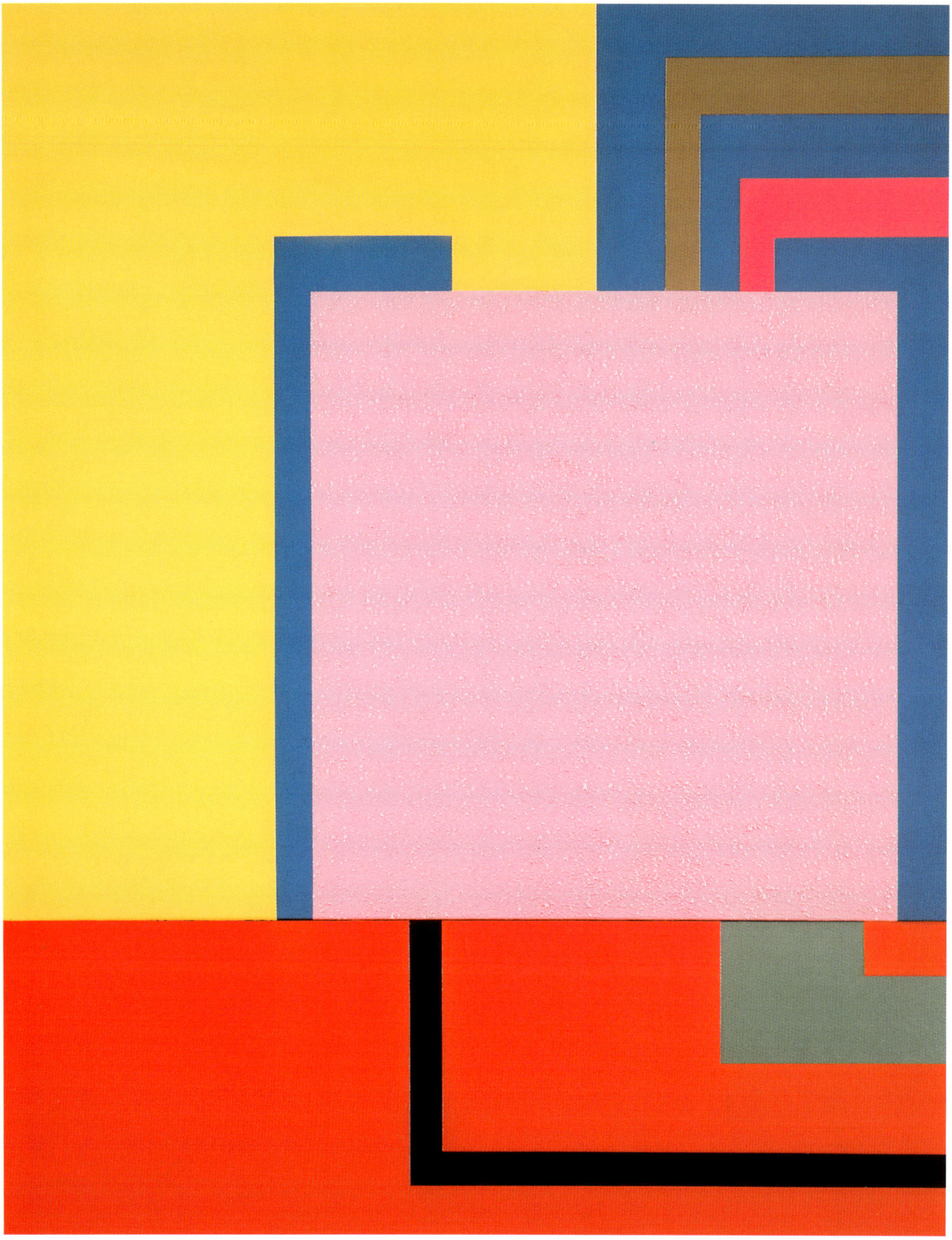

OHNE TITEL / UNTITLED

1999

ACRYL, METALLISCH GLÄNZENDES ACRYL UND ROLL-A-TEX AUF LEINWAND · 160 X 127 CM
ACRYLIC, METALLIC AND PEARLESCENT ACRYLIC AND ROLL-A-TEX ON CANVAS · 63 X 50 IN.

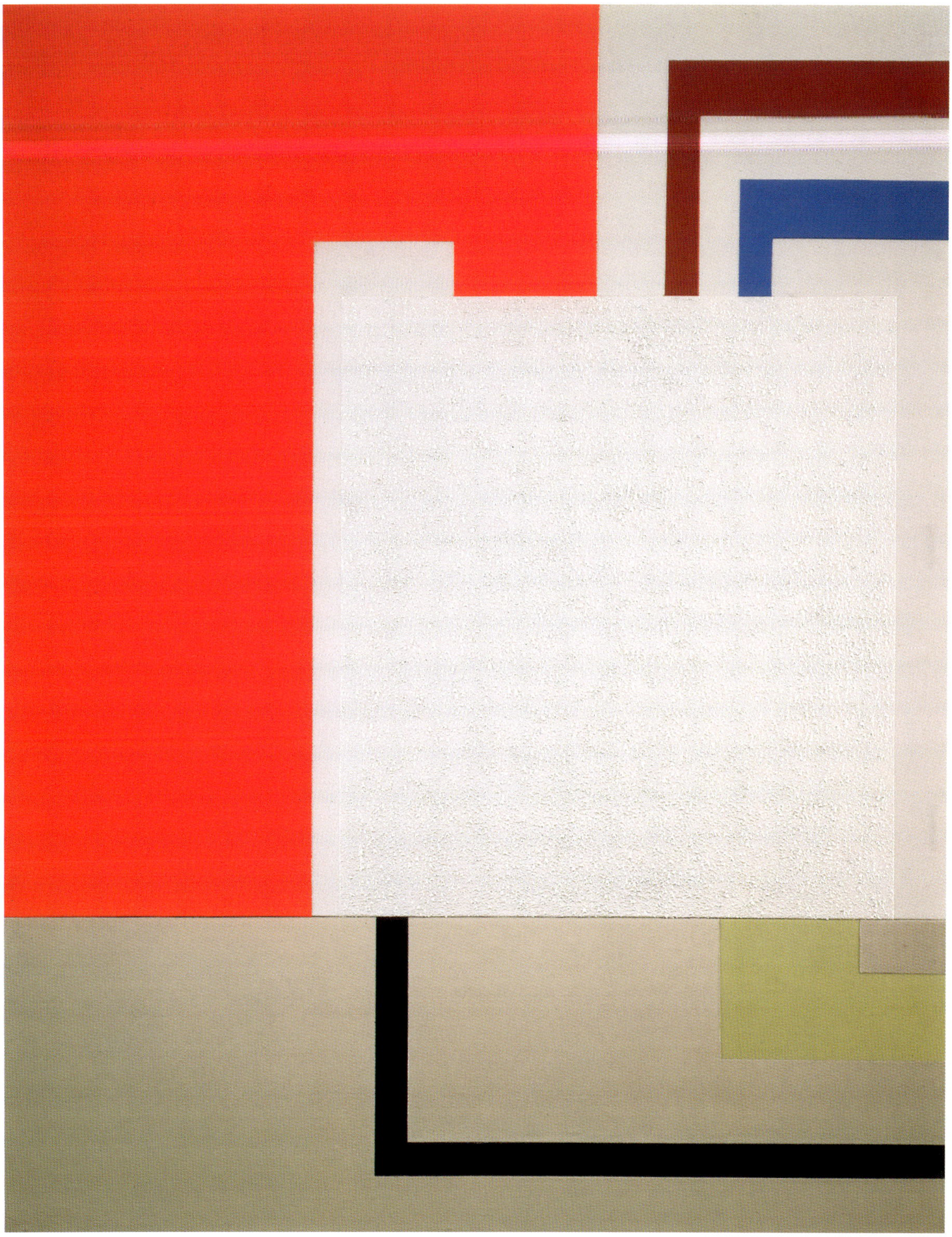

OHNE TITEL / UNTITLED

1999

ACRYL, DAY-GLO, METALLISCHES ACRYL UND ROLL-A-TEX AUF LEINWAND · 160 X 127 CM

ACRYLIC, DAY-GLO AND METALLIC ACRYLIC AND ROLL-A-TEX ON CANVAS · 63 X 50 IN.

MARY HEILMANN

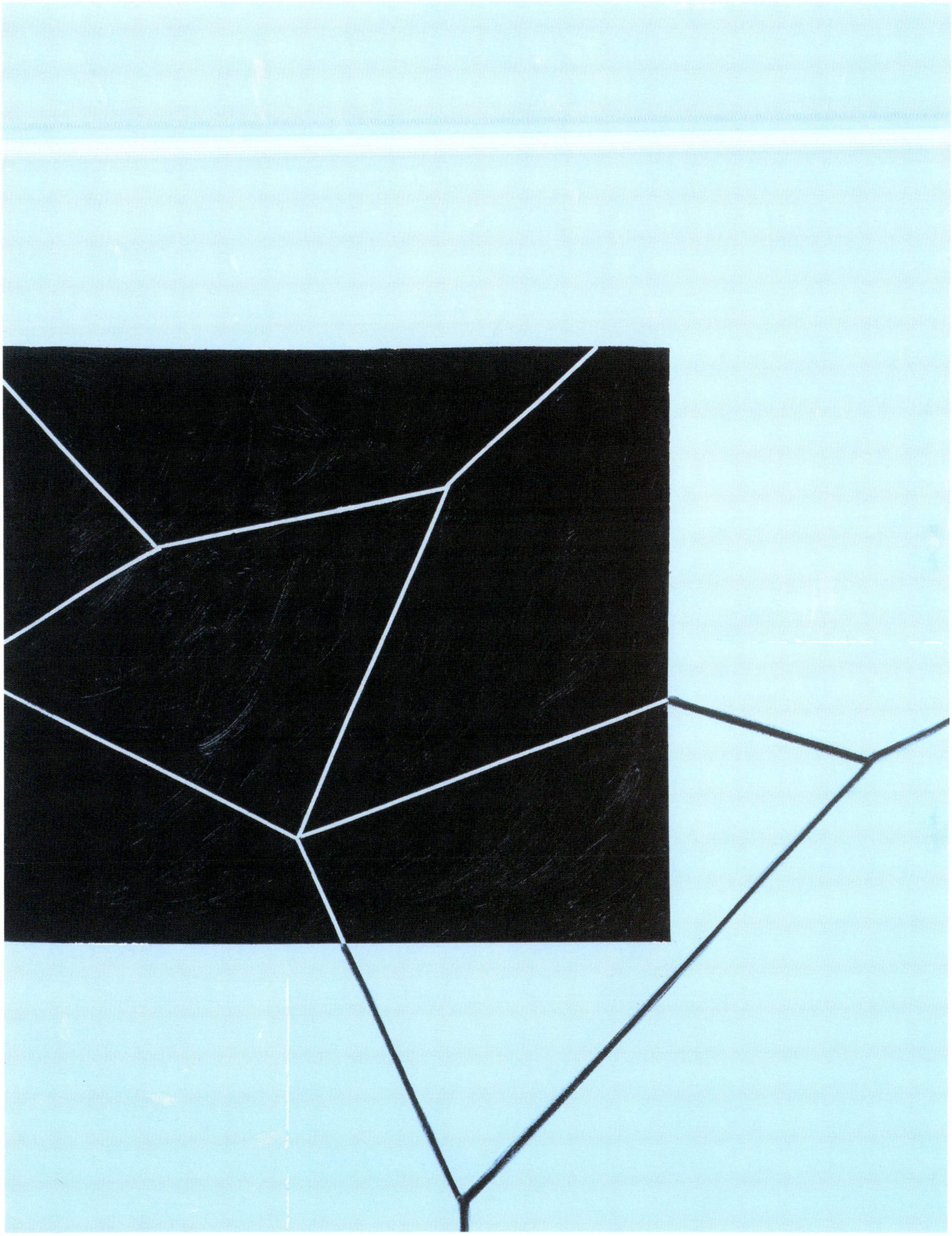

"RUDE BOY"
1998
ÖL AUF LEINWAND · 183 X 152 CM
OIL ON CANVAS · 72 X 60 IN.

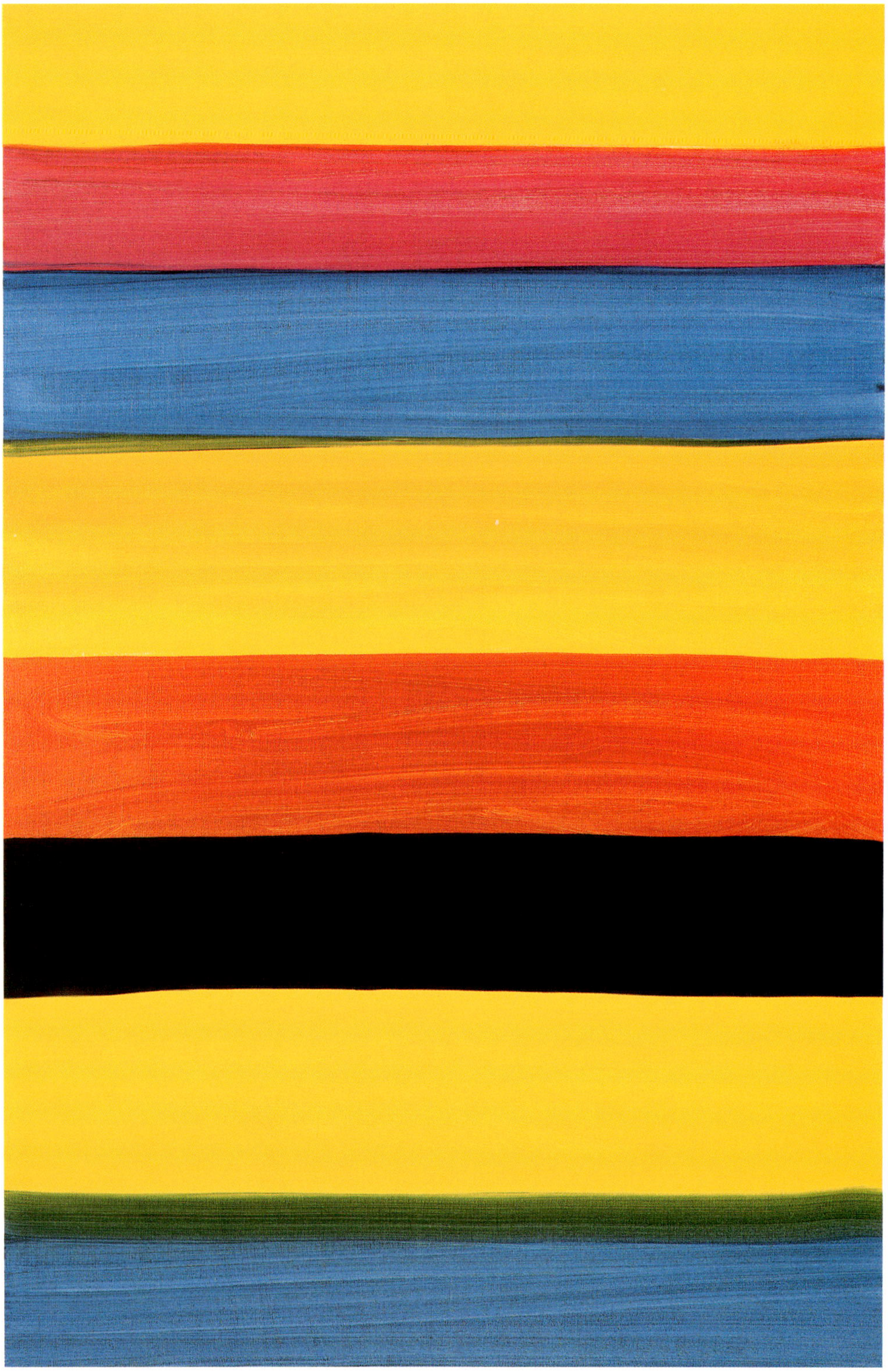

"YELLOW SERAPE"

1993

ÖL AUF LEINWAND · 137 X 91 CM

OIL ON CANVAS · 54 X 36 IN.

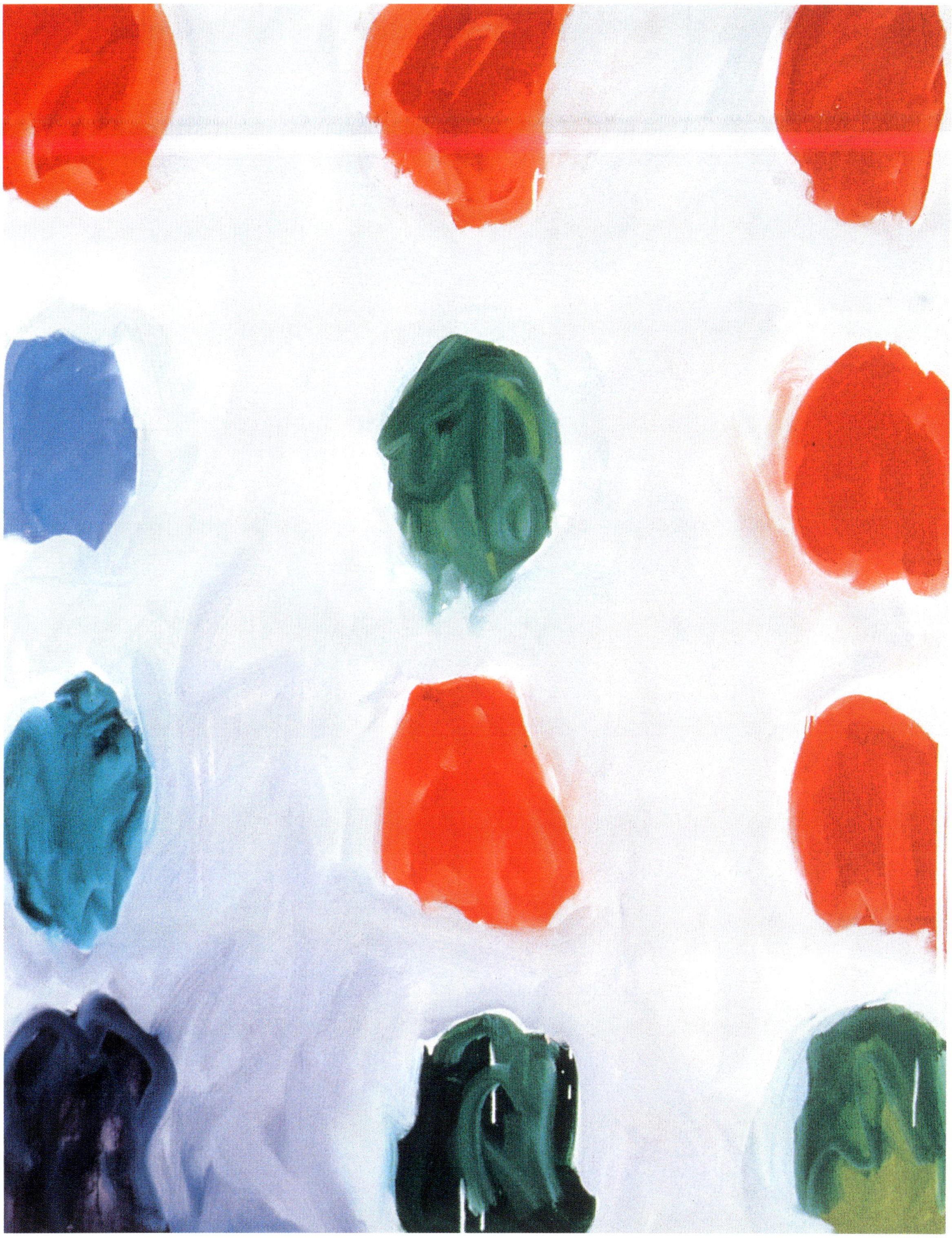

"LAVENDAR BLUE"

1997

ÖL AUF LEINWAND · 127 X 102 CM

OIL ON CANVAS · 50 X 40 IN.

PER KIRKEBY

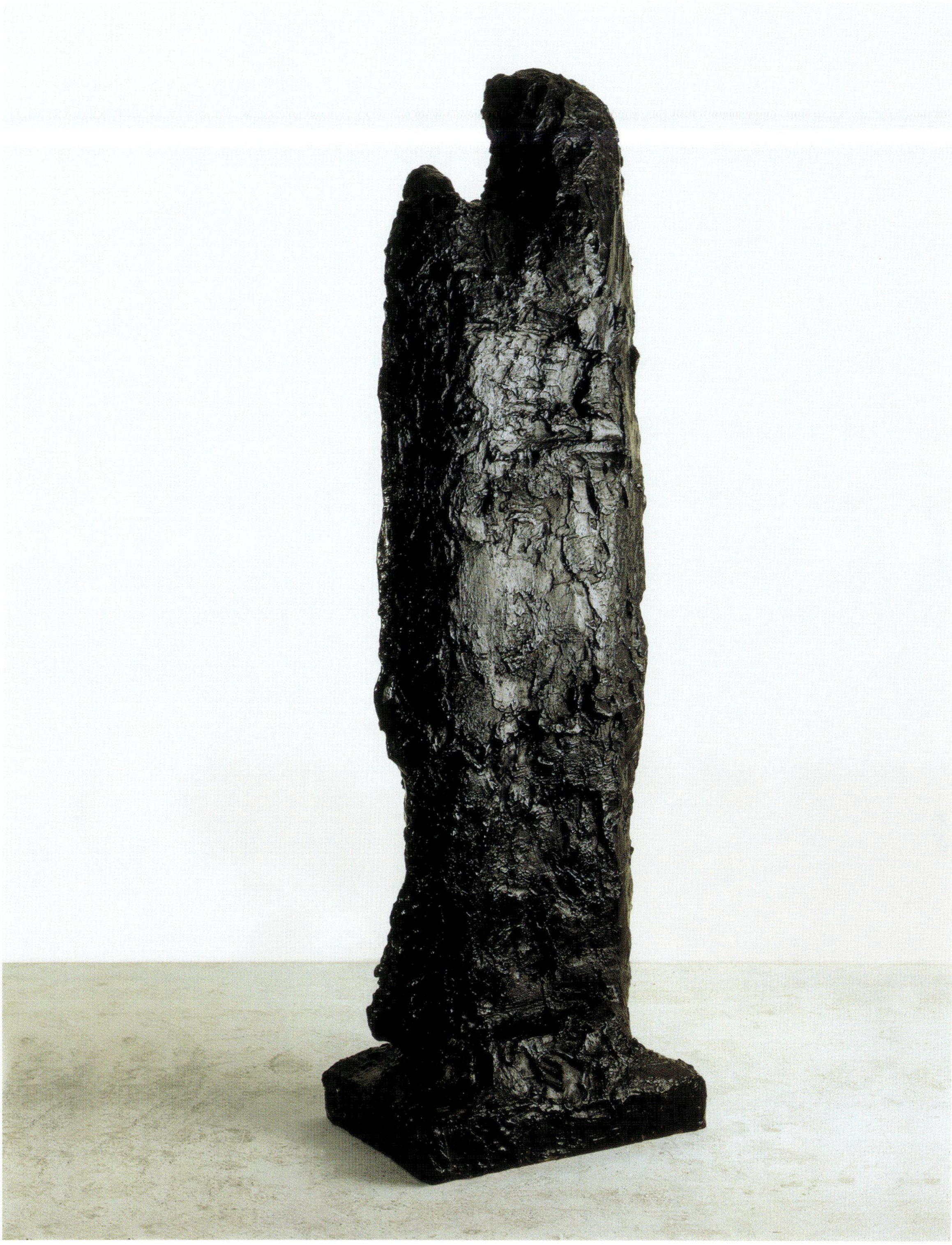

"FIGUR"
1983
BRONZE · 211 X 49 X 68 CM
BRONZE · 83 X 19 X 26,7 IN.

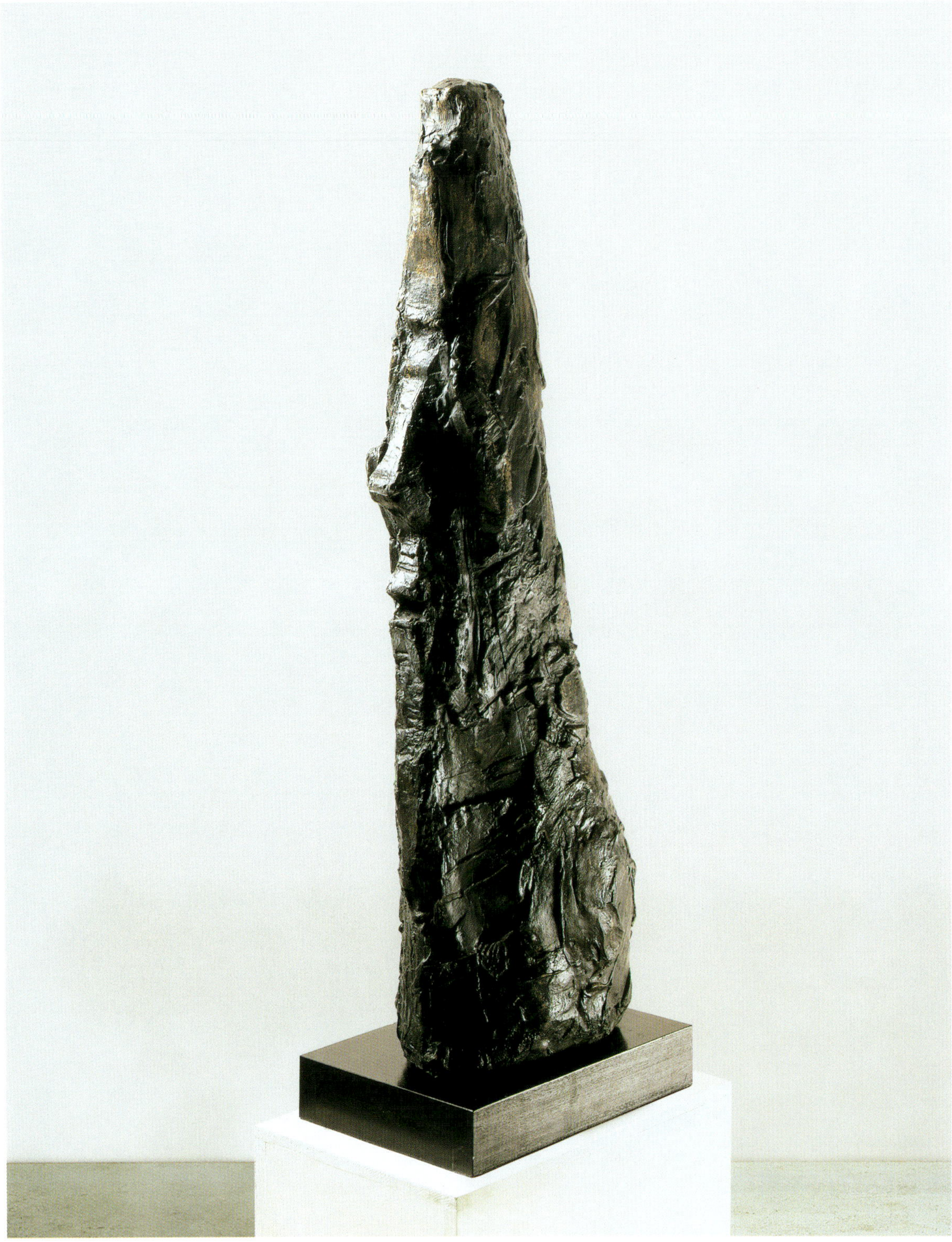

"LAESO - KOPF I"
1983
BRONZE · 83 X 27 X 55 CM
BRONZE · 33 X 10,6 X 21,6 IN.

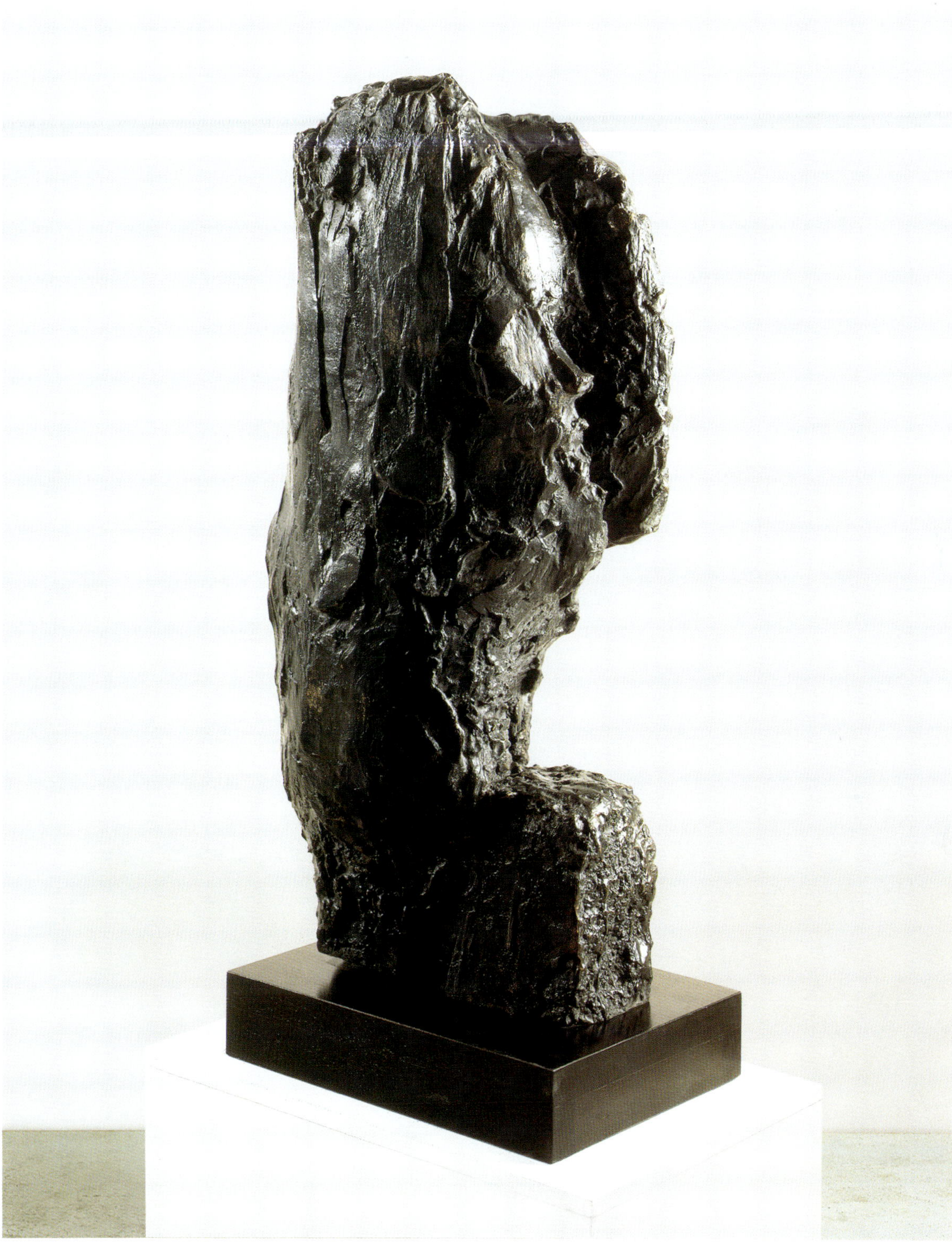

"ARM UND KOPF IV"
1983
BRONZE · 122 X 25 X 47 CM
BRONZE · 48 X 9,8 X 18,5 IN.

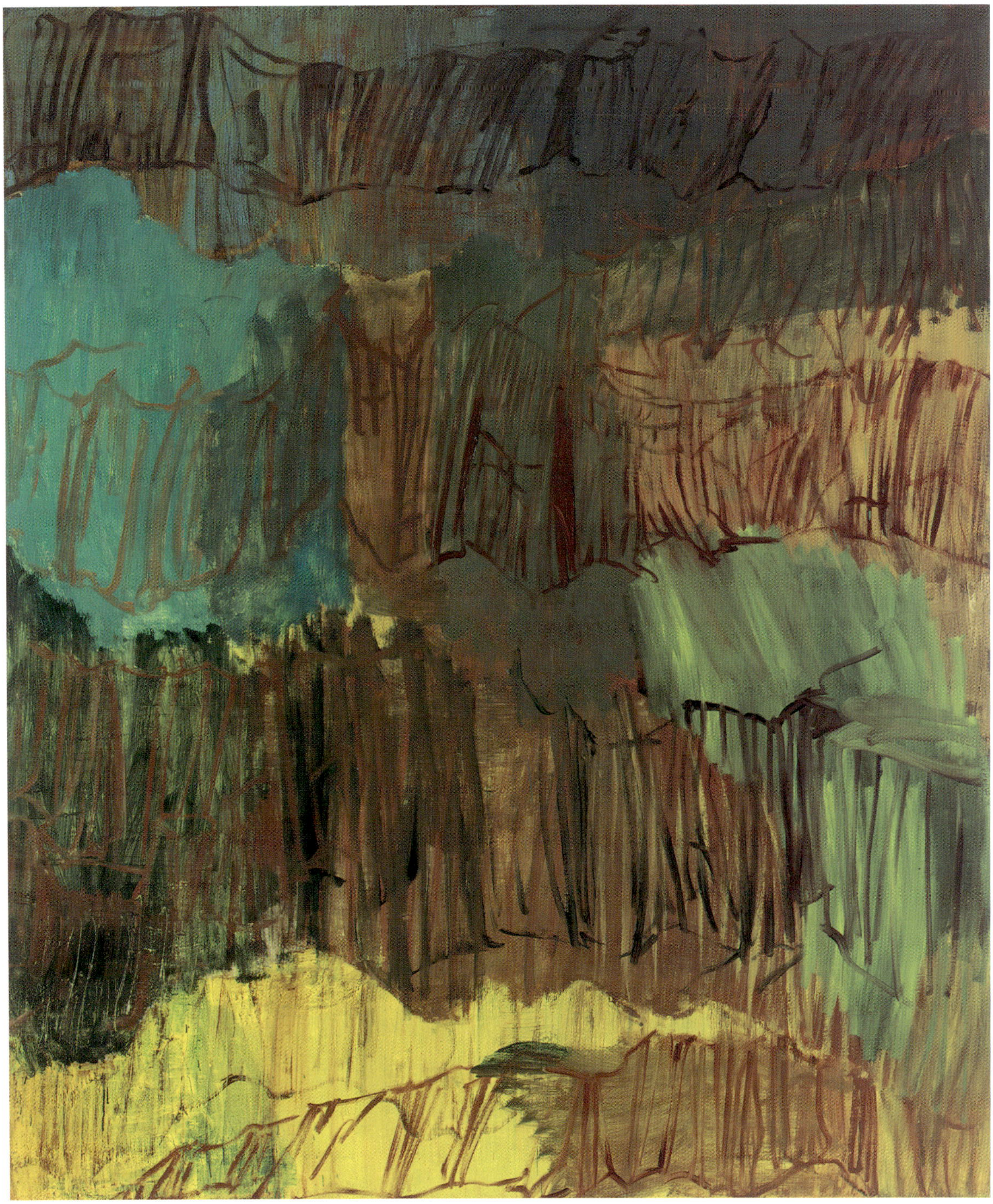

"HERBST -ANASTASIS III"
1997
ÖL AUF LEINWAND · 200 X 170 CM
OIL ON CANVAS · 78,7 X 67 IN.

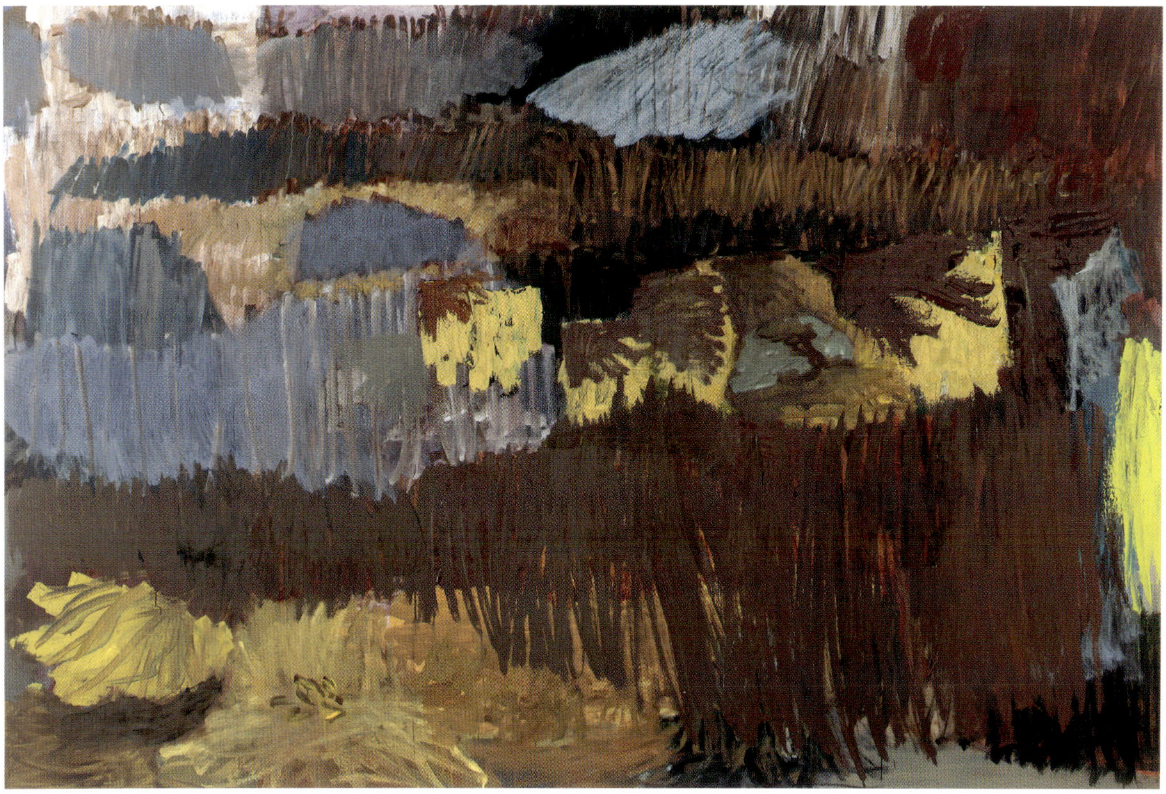

"OHNE TITEL (LAESO)"

1994

ÖL AUF LEINWAND · 200 X 300 CM

OIL ON CANVAS · 78,7 X 118 IN.

IMI KNOEBEL

"JENA 7A"

1996

ACRYL AUF ALUMINIUM · 125,5 X 125 X 5,4 CM

ACRYLIC ON ALUMINIUM · 49,4 X 49,2 X 2,2 IN.

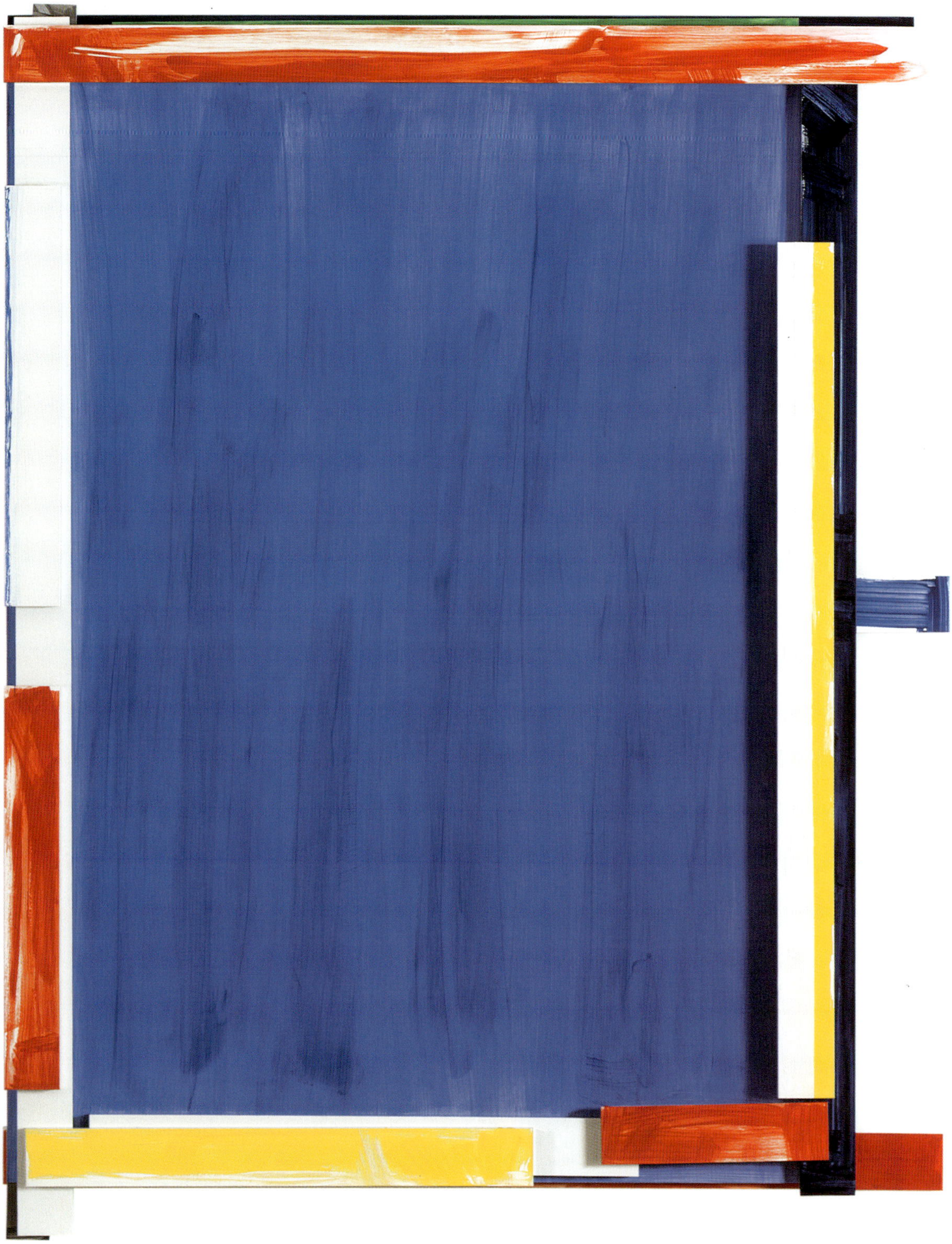

"POINTE DU RAZ"

1998

ACRYL AUF ALUMINIUM · 216 X 176,5 X 8,5 CM

ACRYLIC ON ALUMINIUM · 85 X 69,5 X 3,3 IN.

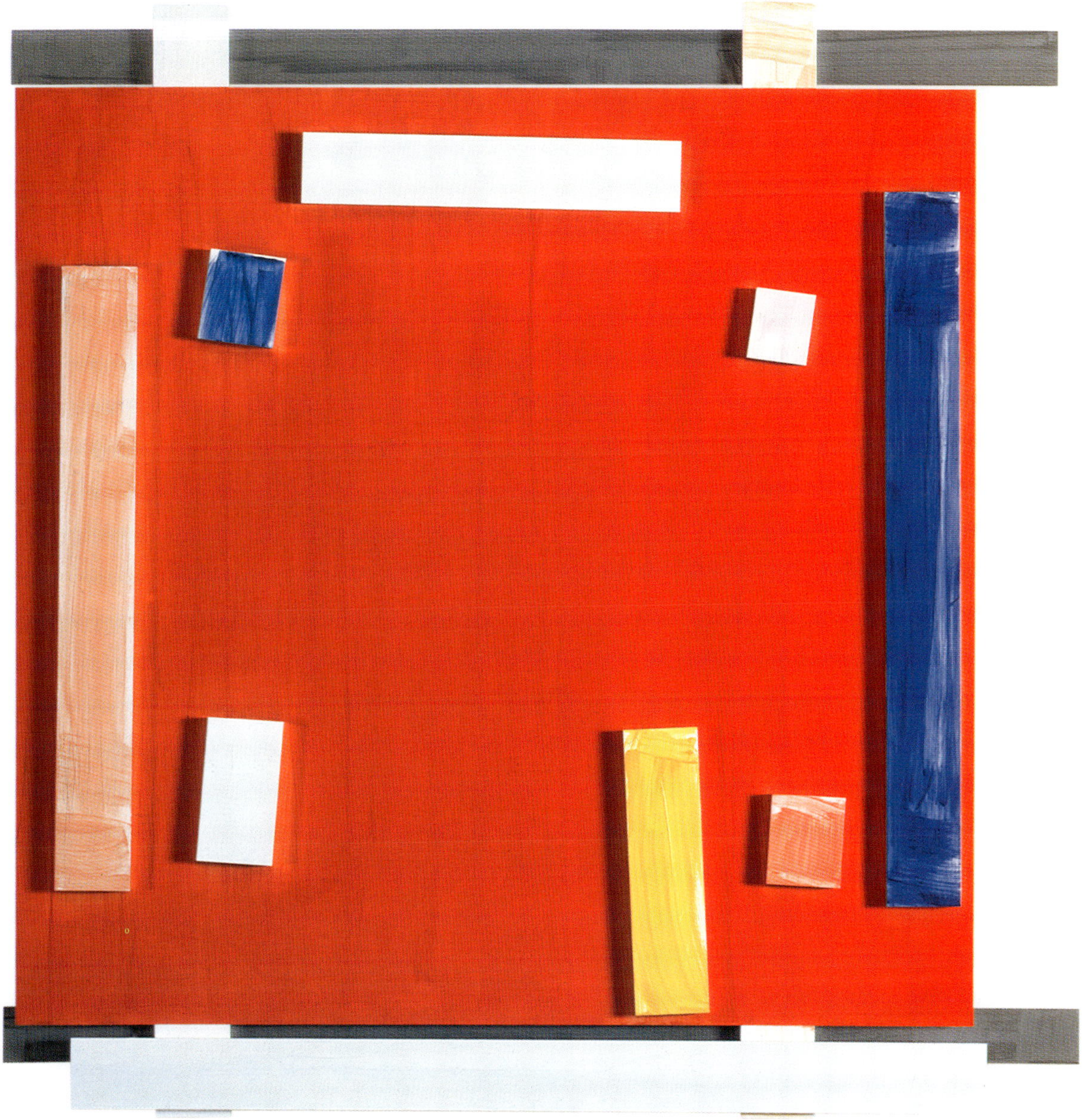

"DIE MOND"

1998

ACRYL AUF ALUMINIUM · 158 X 145,8 X 6,5 CM

ACRYLIC ON ALUMINIUM · 62,2 X 57,4 X 2,5 IN.

JONATHAN LASKER

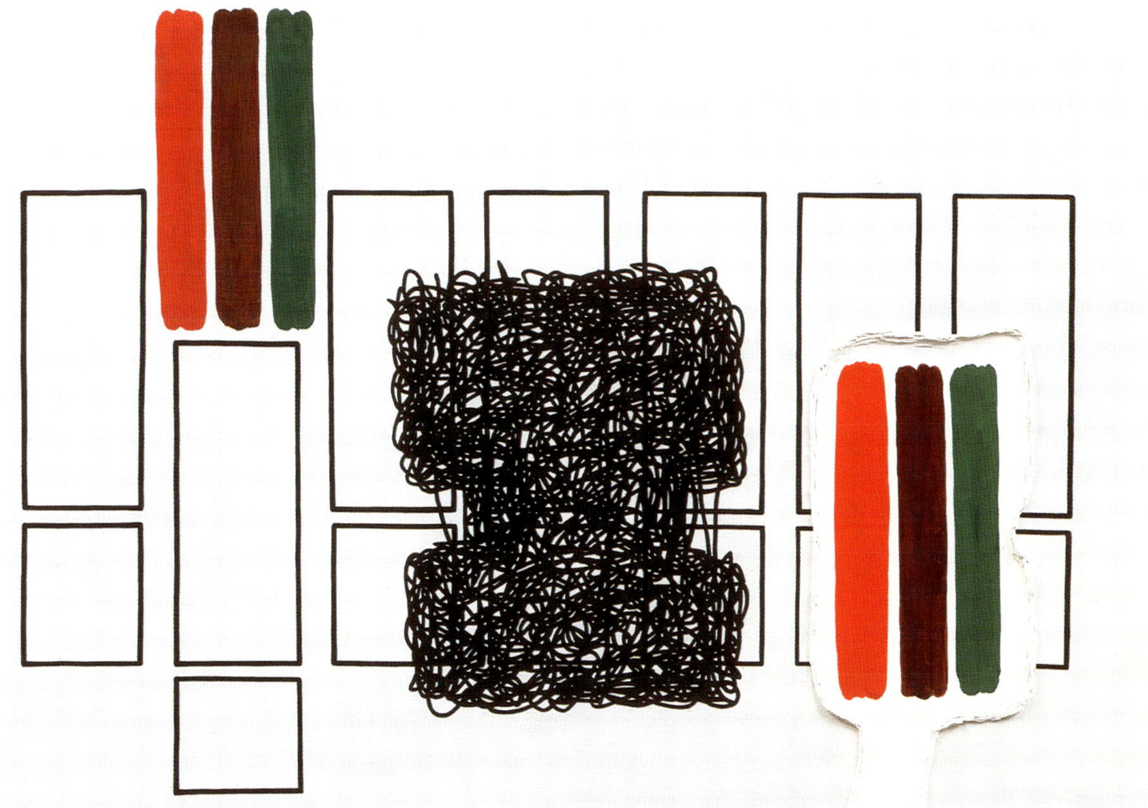

"DAT IS DOT"

1998

ÖL AUF LEINEN · 76 X 102 CM

OIL ON LINEN · 30 X 40 IN.

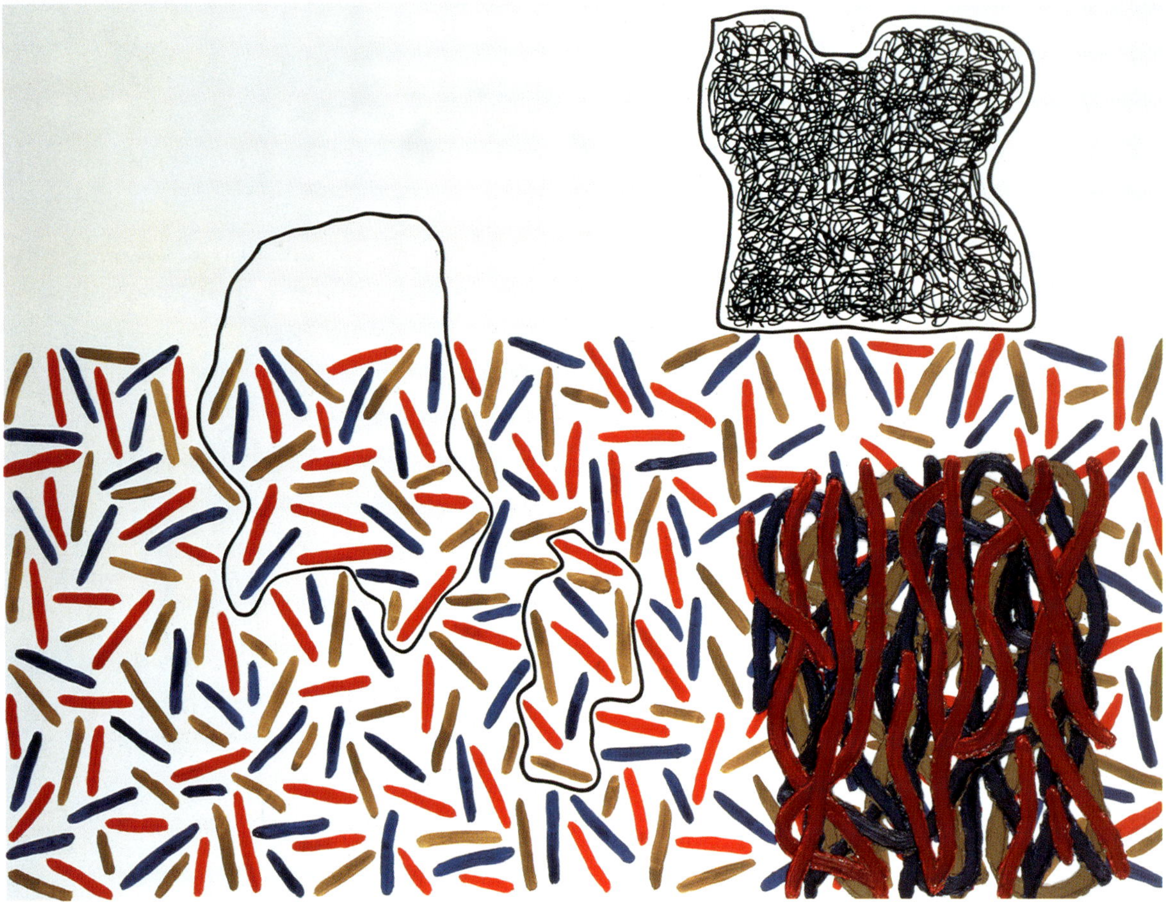

"A FINE DAY IN A WRONG UNIVERSE"
1997
ÖL AUF LEINEN · 160 X 213,4 CM
OIL ON LINEN · 63 X 84 IN.

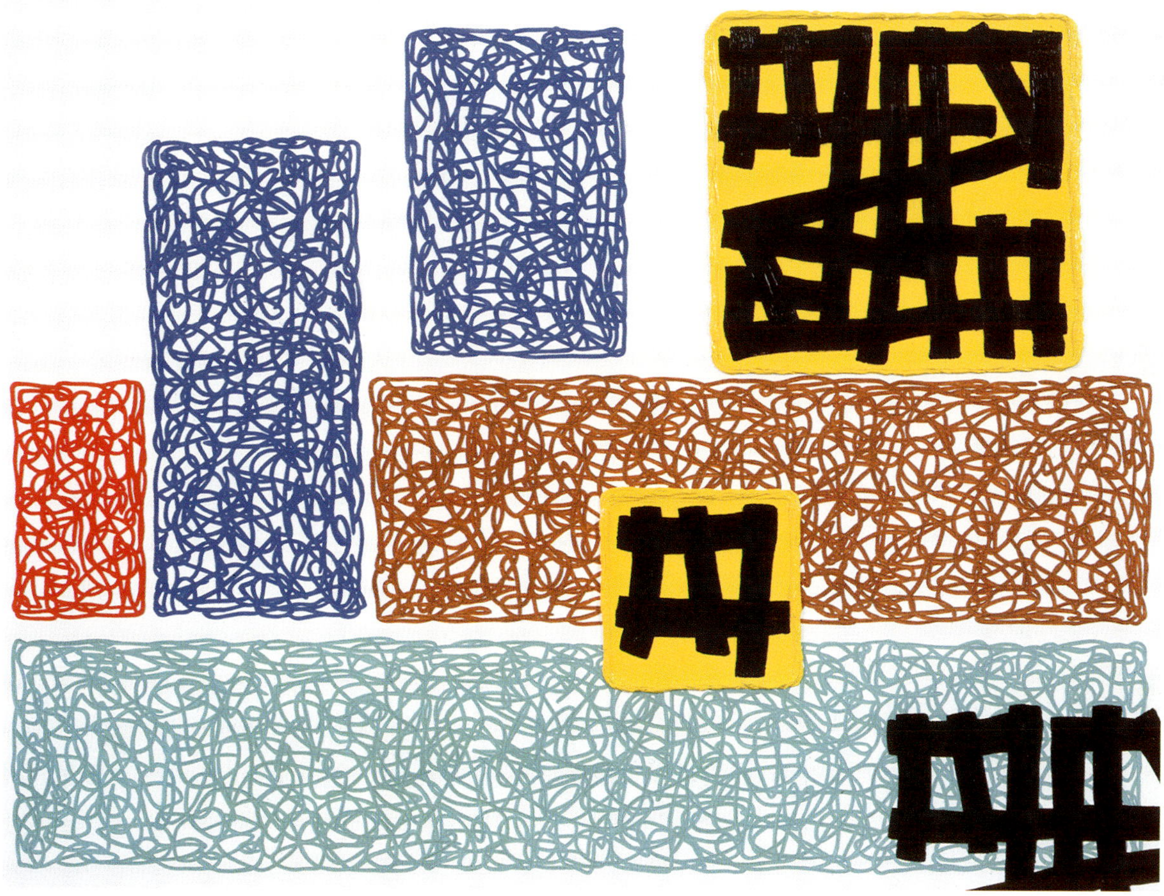

"PERPETUAL PRESENCE"
1999
ÖL AUF LEINEN · 76 X 102 CM
OIL ON LINEN · 30 X 40 IN.

FABIAN MARCACCIO

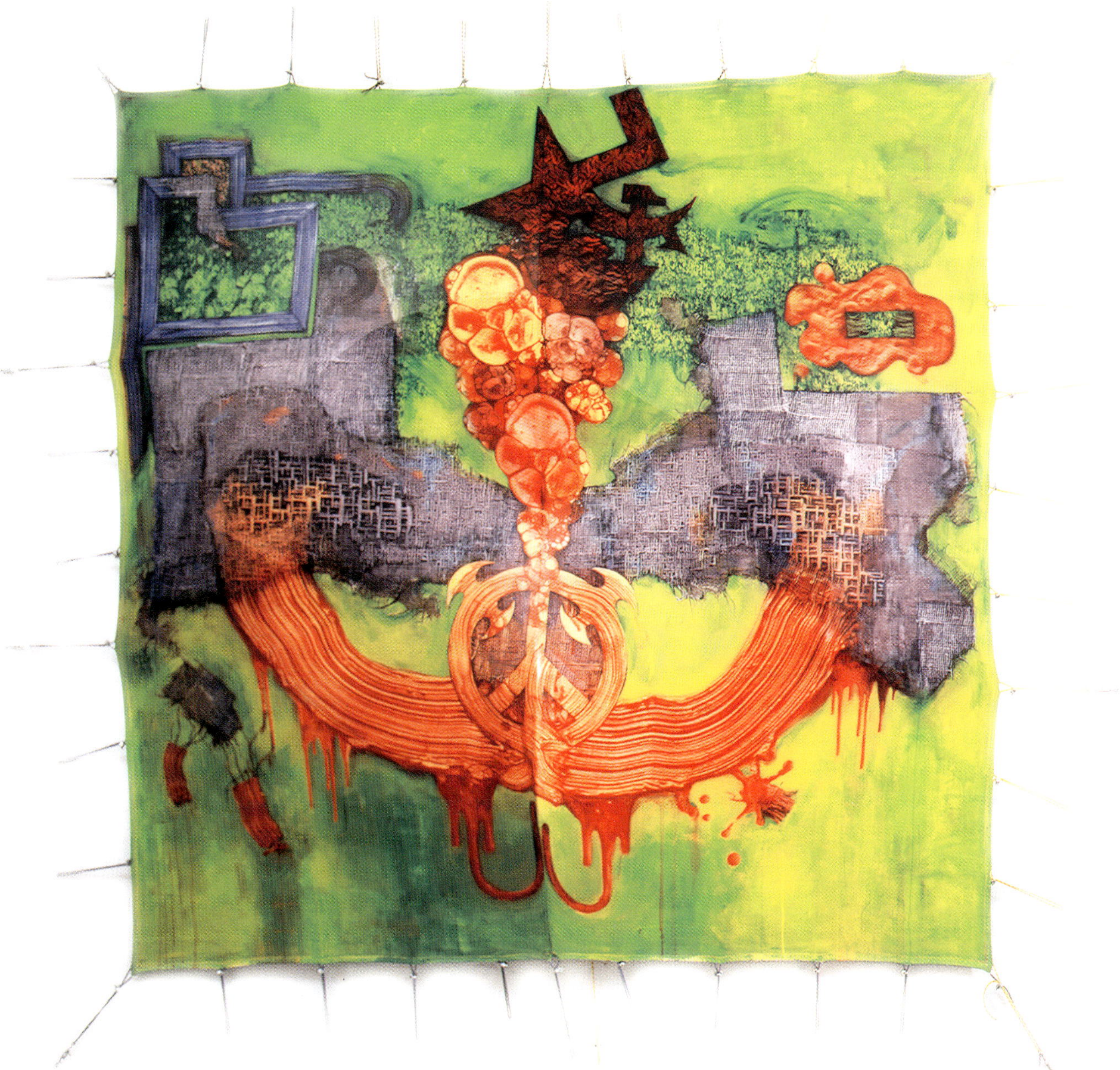

"NEW JUVENILE 2"

1995/96

ÖL UND MISCHTECHNIK AUF LEINWAND · 305 X 305 X 35 CM

OIL AND MIXED MEDIA ON CANVAS · 120 X 120 X 14 IN.

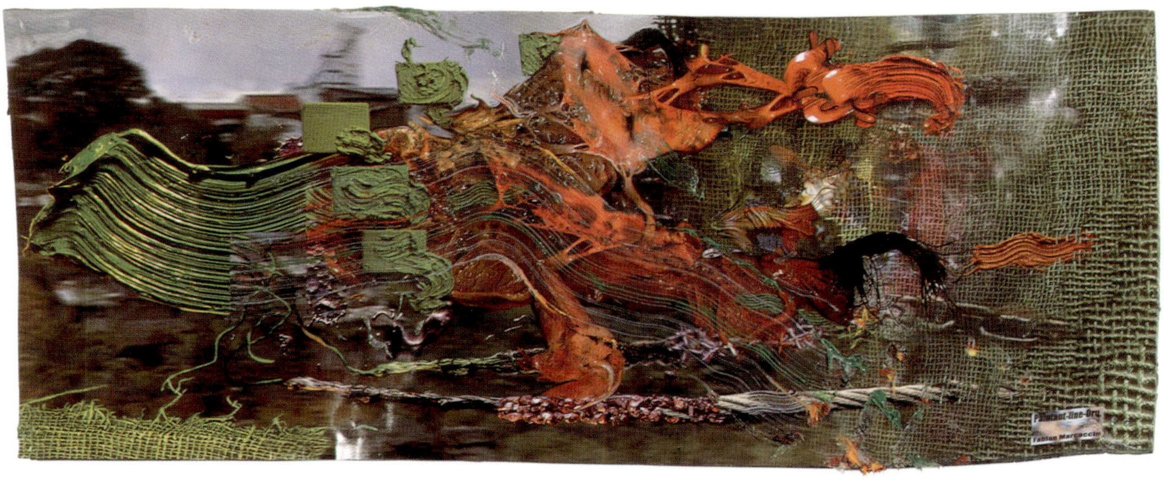

"PAINTED-LINE-ORG"

1999

MISCHTECHNIK AUF VINYL · 99 X 259 X 23 CM

MIXED MEDIA ON VINYL · 39 X 102 X 9 IN.

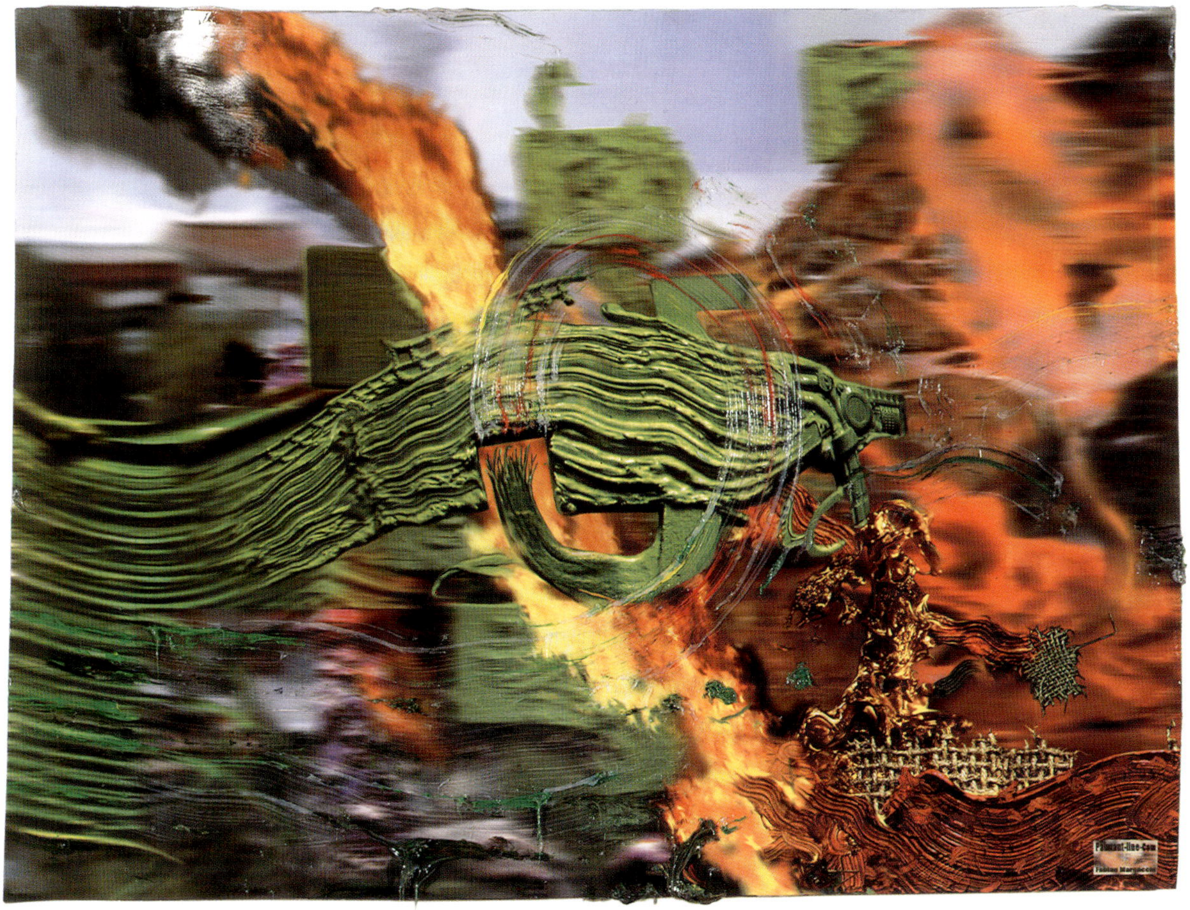

"PAINTED-LINE-COM"

1999

MISCHTECHNIK AUF VINYL · 99 X 132 X 20 CM

MIXED MEDIA ON VINYL · 39 X 52 X 8 IN.

JASON MARTIN

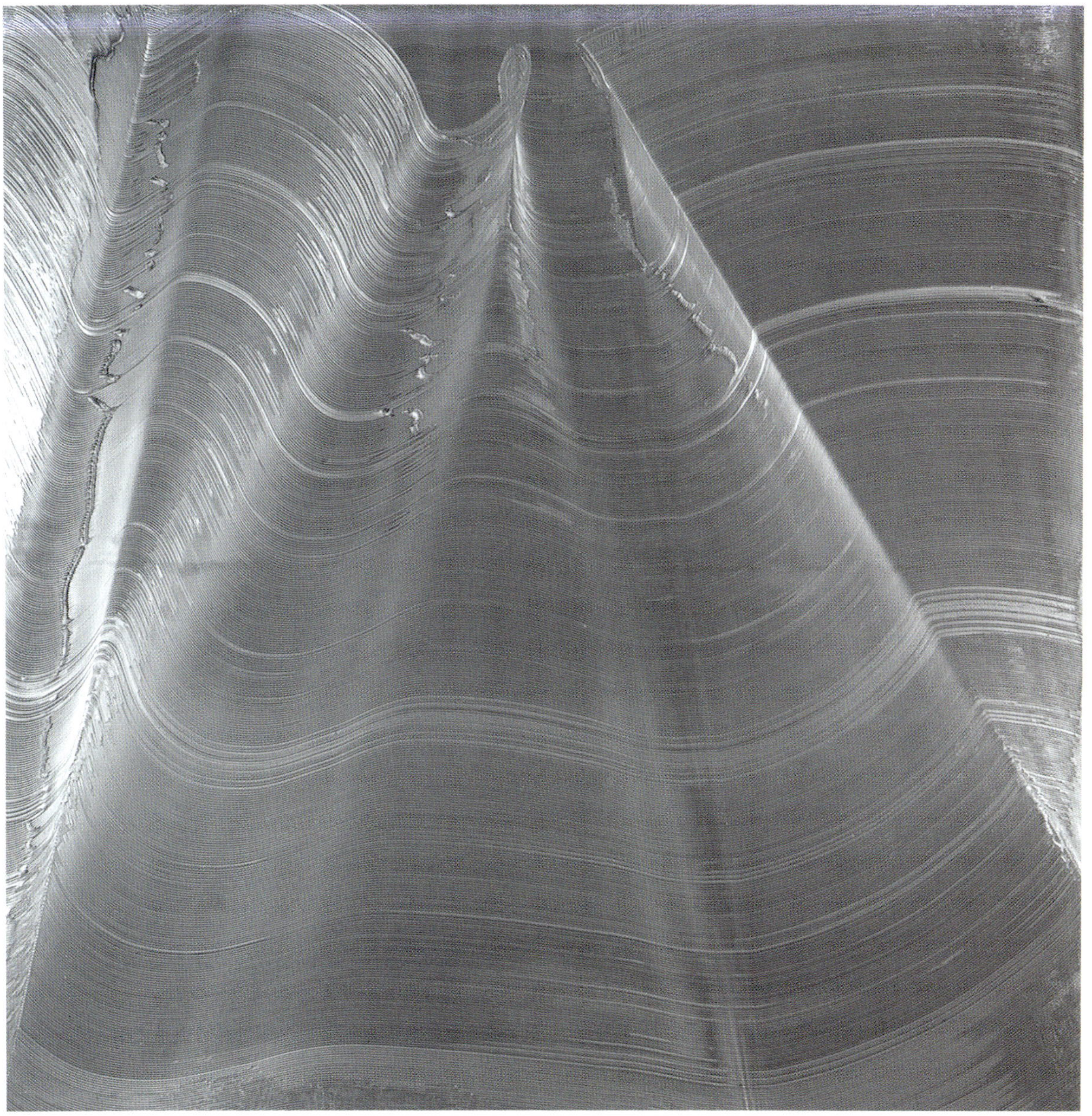

"ANGEL"

1999

ACRYL AUF ALUMINIUM · 180 X 180 X 10 CM

ACRYLIC ON ALUMINIUM · 71 X 71 X 4 IN.

"AVALANCHE"
1998
ÖL AUF PERSPEX · 61 X 61 X 3 CM
OIL ON PERSPEX · 24 X 24 X 1,2 IN.

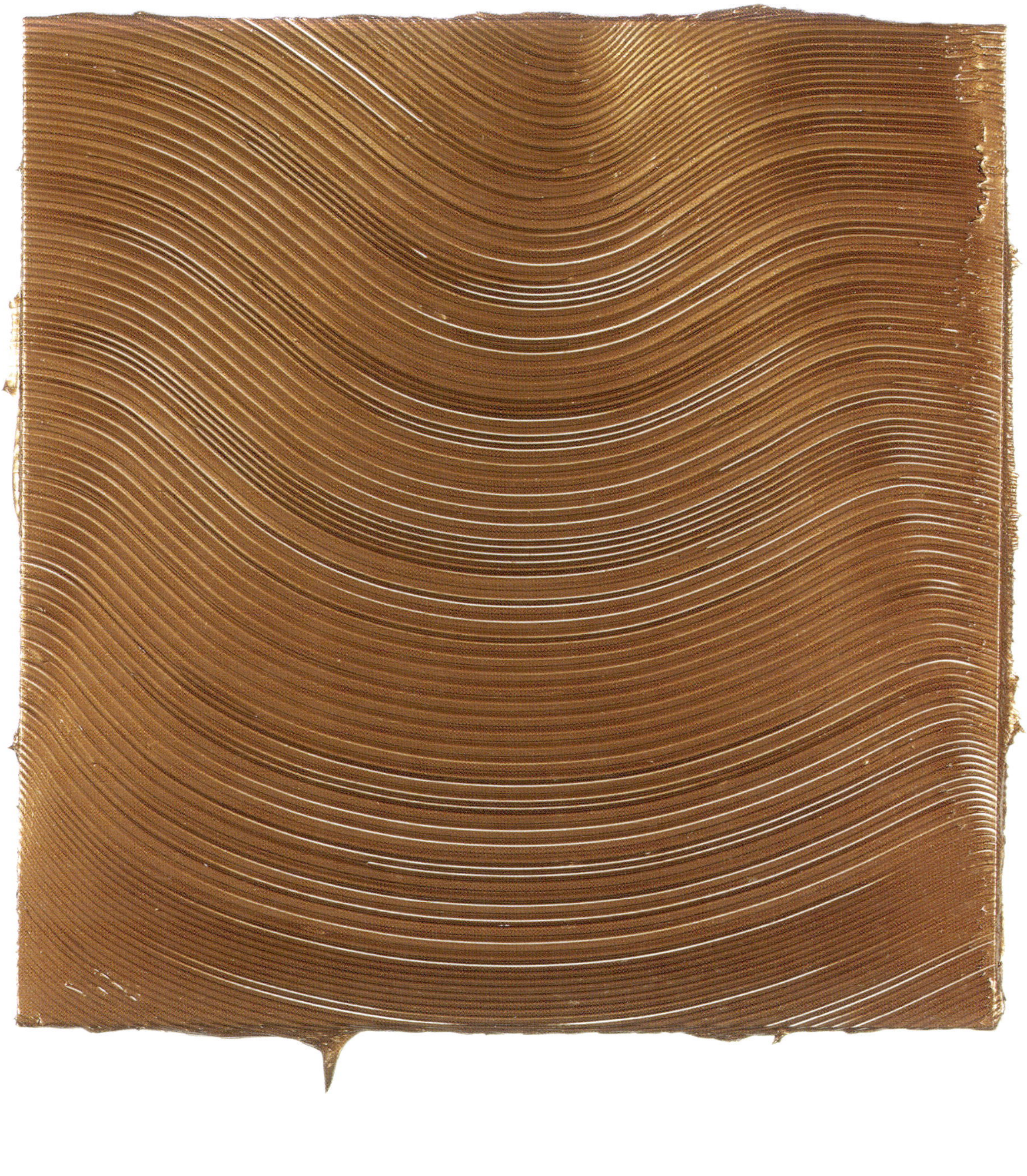

OHNE TITEL / UNTITLED

1998

ACRYL AUF MDF · 40 X 40 X 5 CM

ACRYLIC ON MDF · 15,7 X 15,7 X 2 IN.

WALTER OBHOLZER

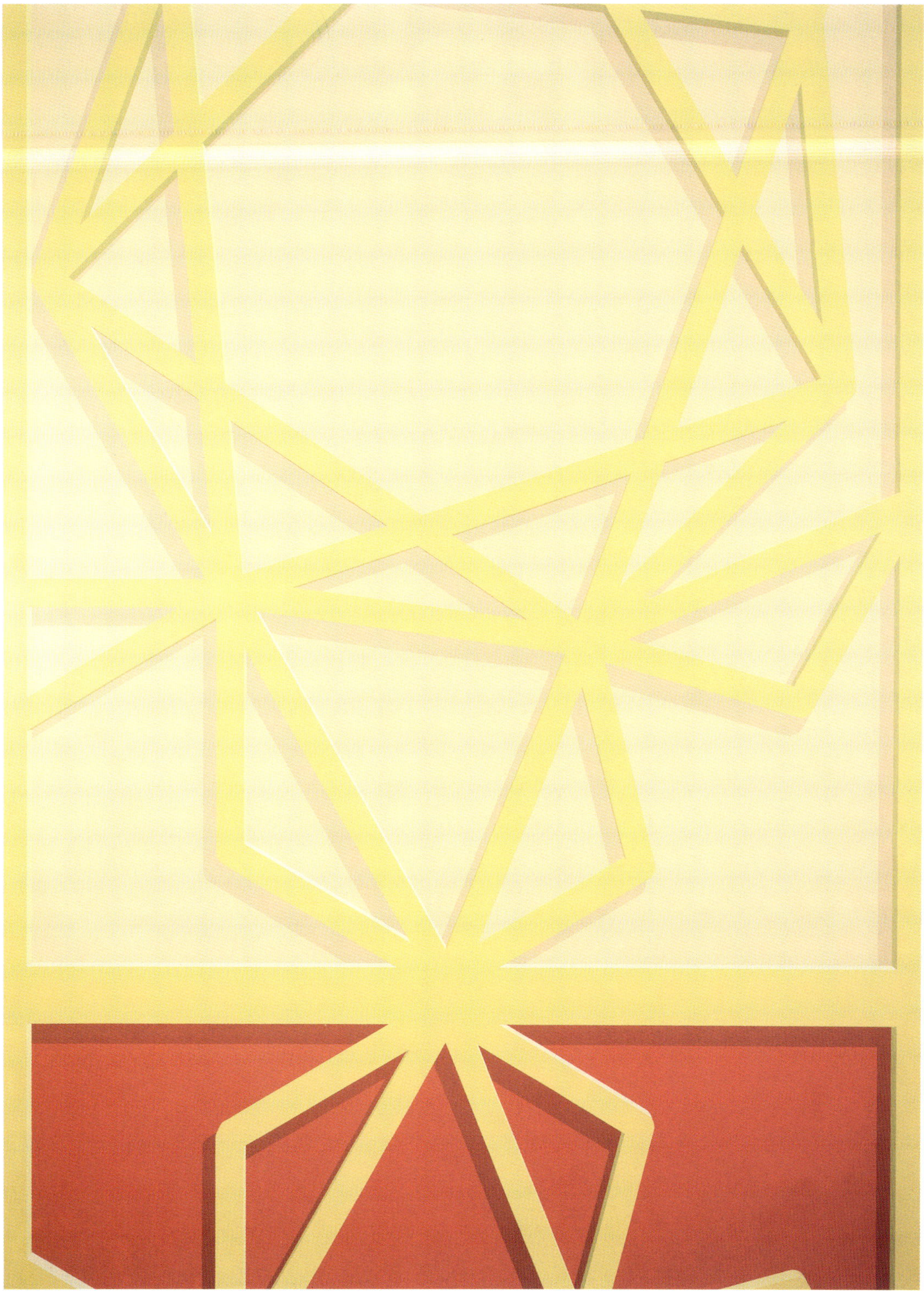

OHNE TITEL / UNTITLED

1998

TEMPERA AUF ALUMINIUM · 211 X 155 CM

TEMPERA ON ALUMINIUM · 83 X 61 IN.

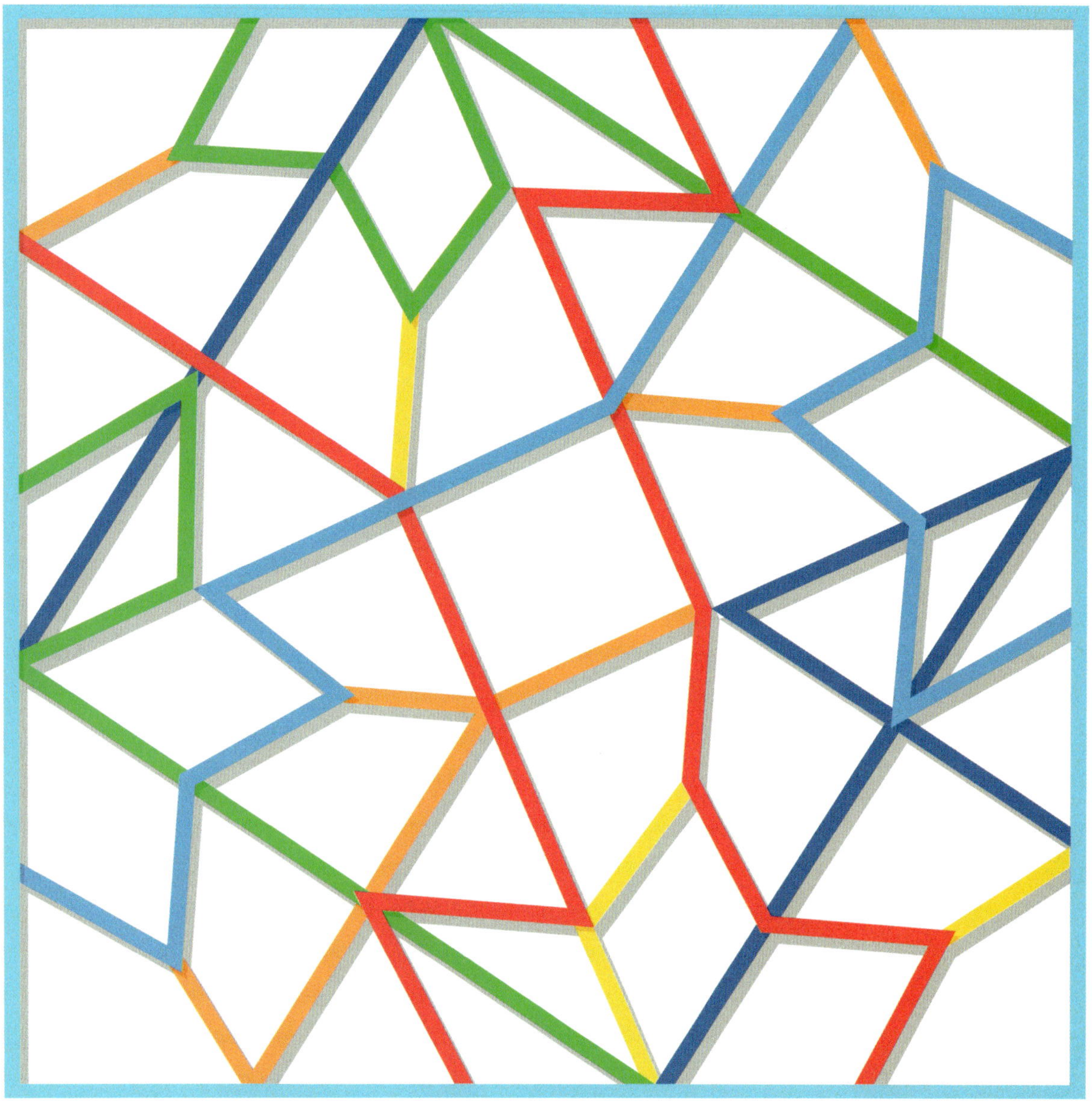

"OTAKU 4"

1998

TEMPERA AUF ALUMINIUM · 180 X 185 CM

TEMPERA ON ALUMINIUM · 70,8 X 72,8 IN.

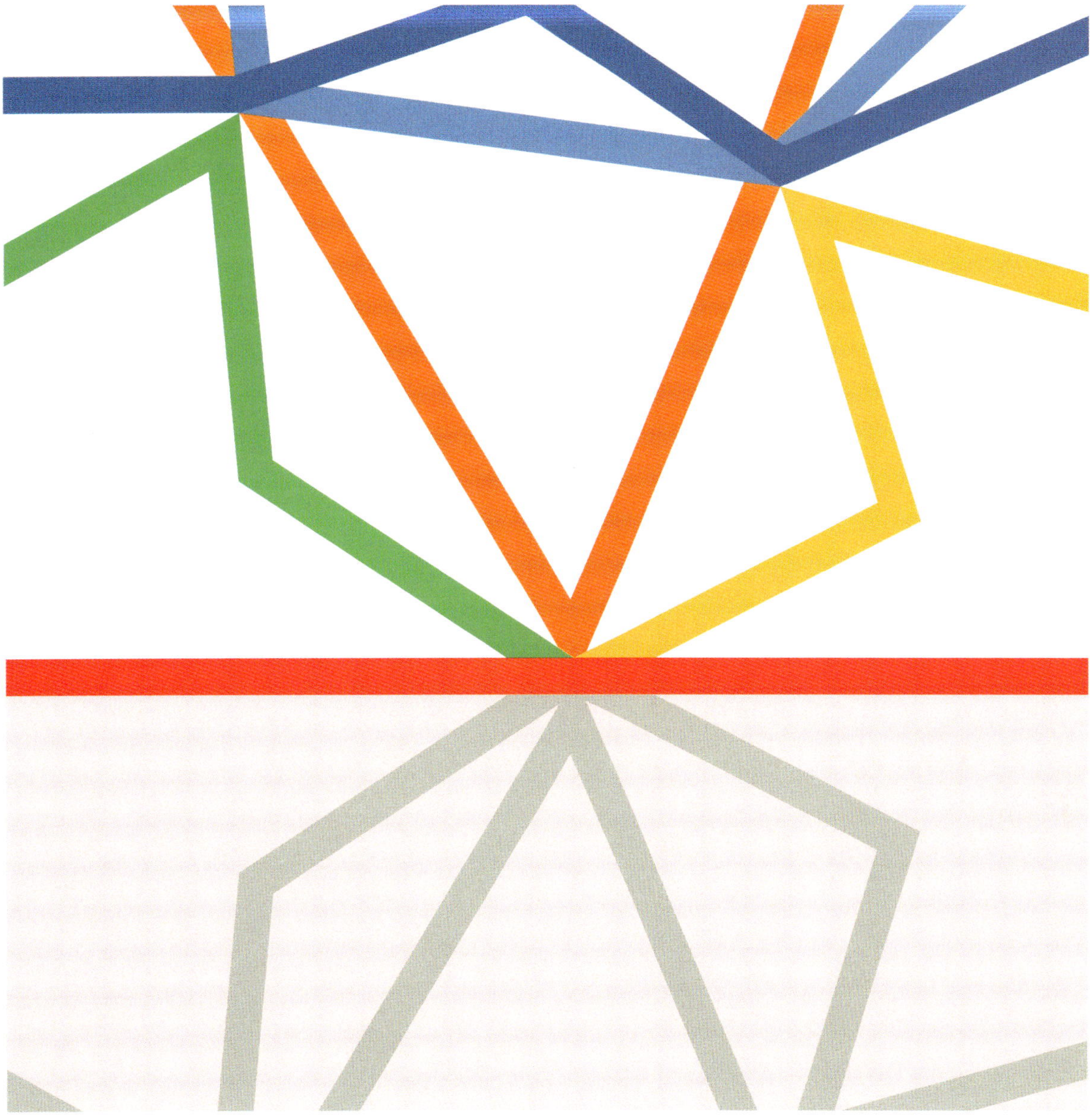

"DETAIL NR.10"

1999

TEMPERA AUF ALUMINIUM · 109 X 109 CM

TEMPERA ON ALUMINIUM · 43 X 43 IN.

DAVID REED

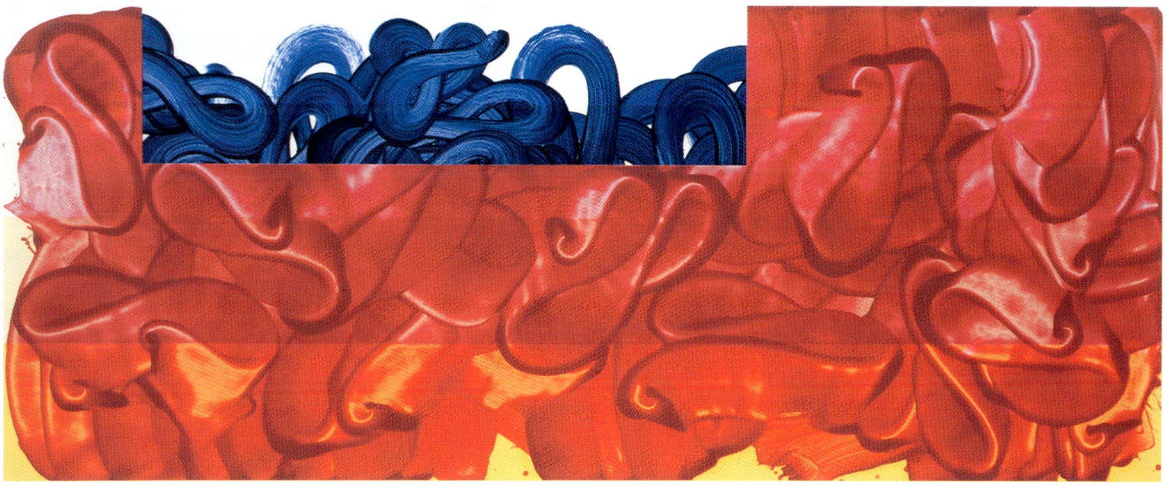

"#440"

1998/99

ÖL UND ALKYD AUF LEINEN · 132 X 330 CM

OIL AND ALKYD ON LINEN · 52 X 130 IN.

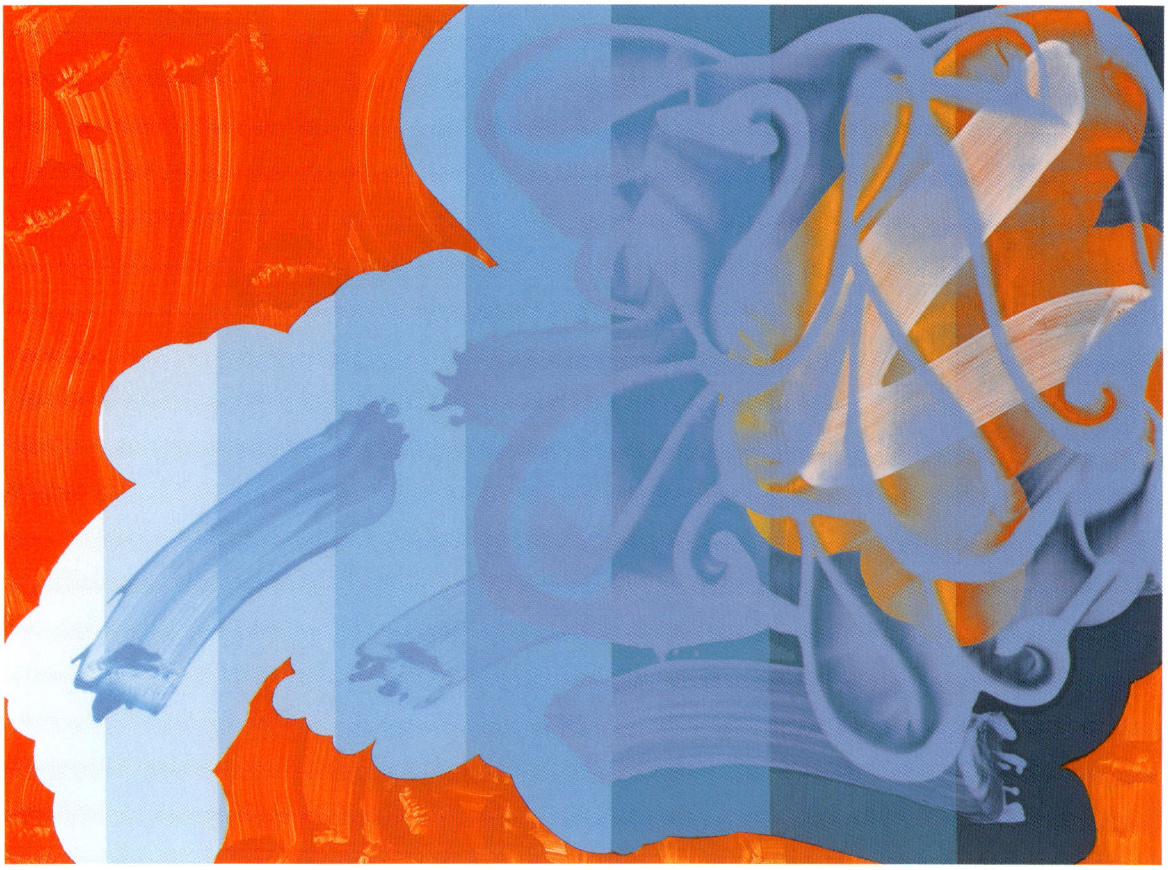

"#407"

1997/98

ÖL UND ALKYD AUF METALL · 81 X 112 CM

OIL AND ALKYD ON LINEN · 32 X 44 IN.

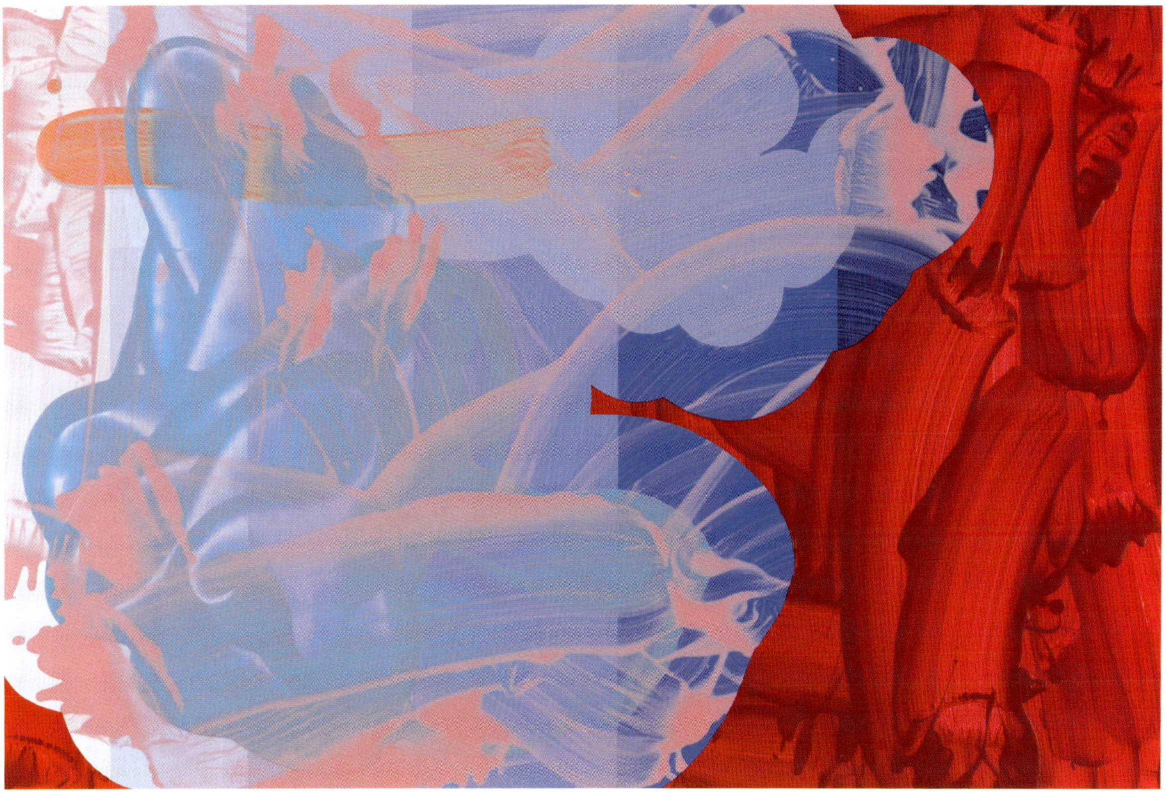

"#415"

1998
ÖL UND ALKYD AUF METALL · 71 X 107 CM
OIL AND ALKYD ON LINEN · 28 X 42 IN.

GERHARD RICHTER

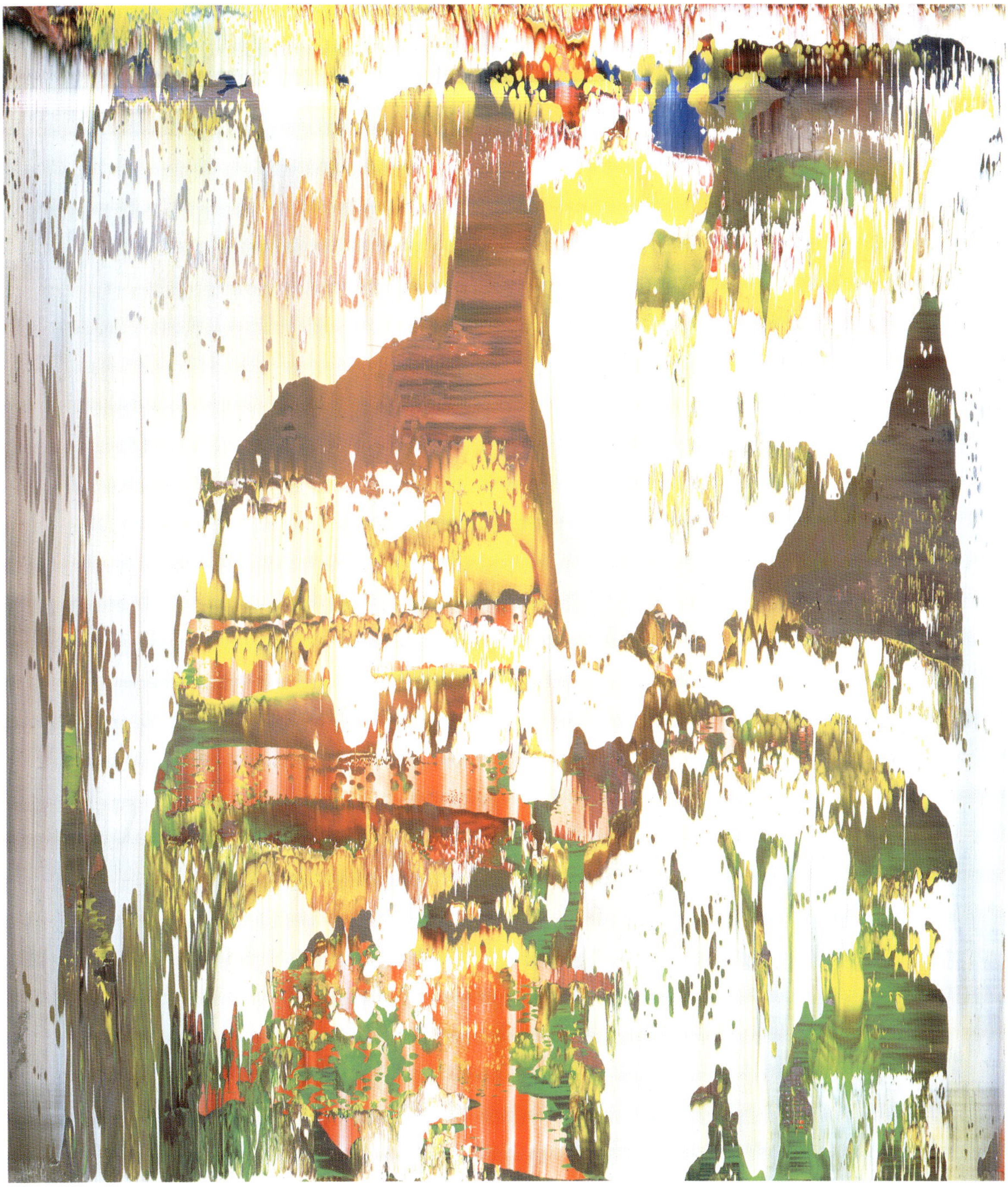

"ABSTRAKTES BILD (843-6)"

1997

ÖL AUF ALUMINIUM · 55 X 48 CM

OIL ON ALUMINIUM · 21,6 X 19 IN.

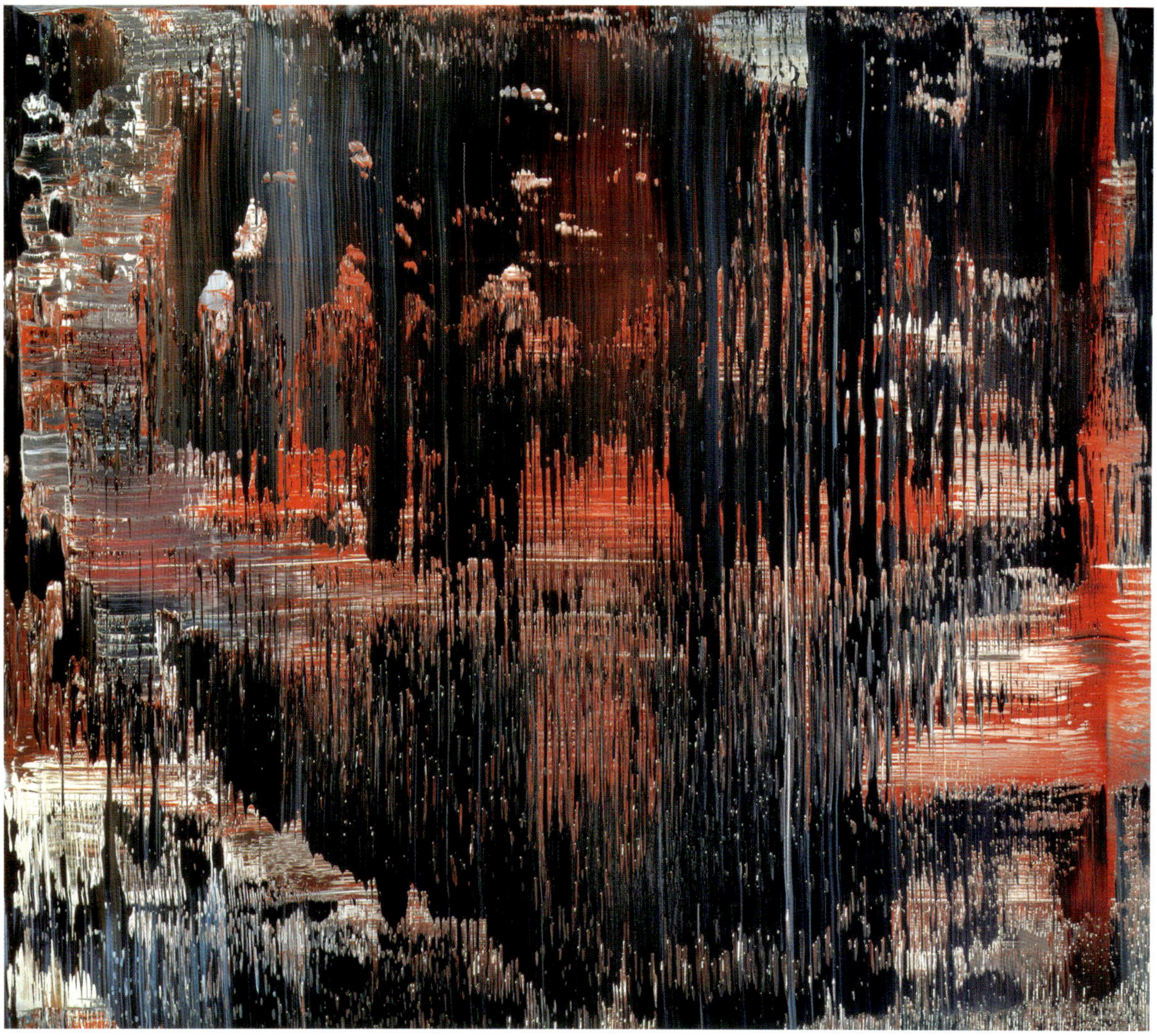

"ABSTRAKTES BILD (842-8)"
1997
ÖL AUF ALUMINIUM · 48 X 55 CM
OIL ON ALUMINIUM · 19 X 21,6 IN.

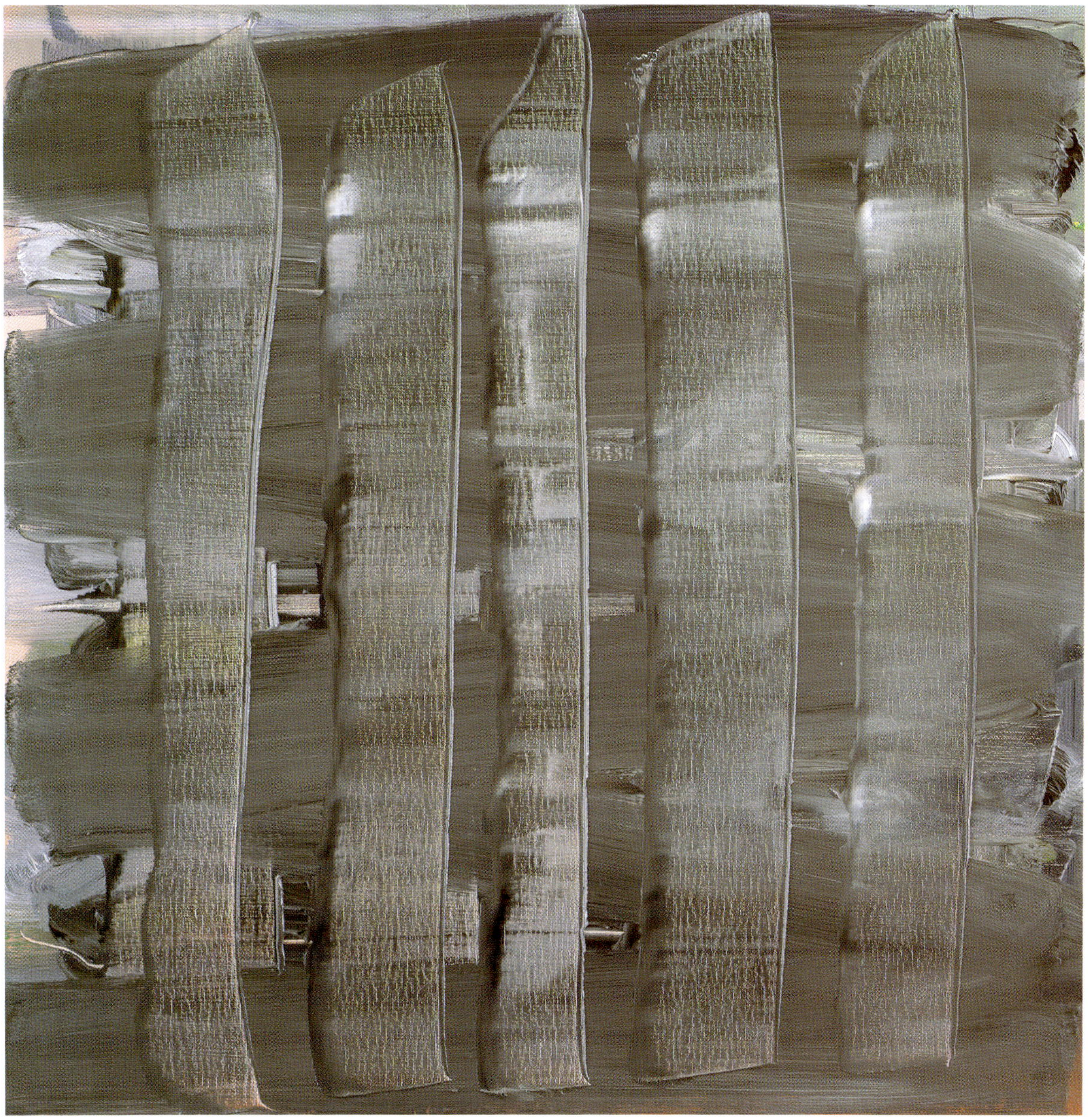

"ABSTRAKTES BILD (755-3)"

1992

ÖL AUF LEINWAND · 61 X 61 CM

OIL ON CANVAS · 24 X 24 IN.

HUBERT SCHEIBL

"OMIAI-O"

1995/96
ÖL AUF LEINWAND · 250 X 200 CM
OIL ON CANVAS · 98,4 X 78,7 IN.

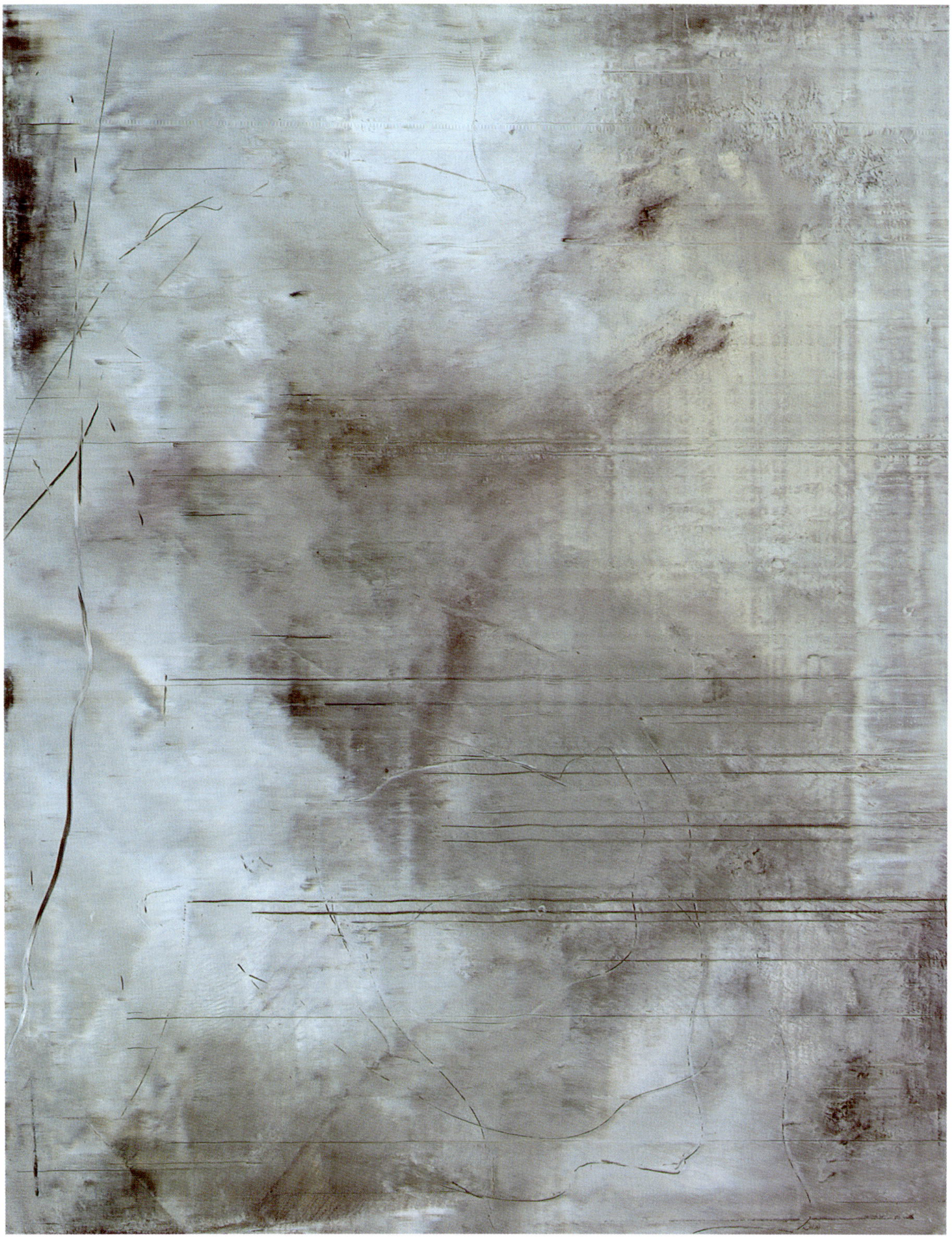

"STRANGE DAYS"
1998/99
ÖL AUF LEINWAND · 200 X 150 CM
OIL ON CANVAS · 78,7 X 59 IN.

"B.O.W. -3"

1994/95

ÖL AUF LEINWAND · 250 X 250 CM

OIL ON CANVAS · 98,4 X 98,4 IN.

GÜNTER UMBERG

OHNE TITEL / UNTITLED

1998

POLIMER, PIGMENT UND DAMMAR AUF HOLZ · 53 X 48 CM

POLYMER, PIGMENT AND DAMMAR ON WOOD · 20,8 X 19 IN.

OHNE TITEL / UNTITLED

1998

POLIMER, PIGMENT UND DAMMAR AUF HOLZ · ZWEITEILIG, JE 32 X 57 CM

POLYMER, PIGMENT AND DAMMAR ON WOOD IN TWO SECTIONS · 12,6 X 22,4 IN.

OHNE TITEL / UNTITLED

1991-92 / 1995-98
PIGMENT UND DAMMAR AUF HOLZ · 180 X 61 X 4 CM
PIGMENT AND DAMMAR ON WOOD · 70,8 X 24 X 1,6 IN.

JUAN USLÉ

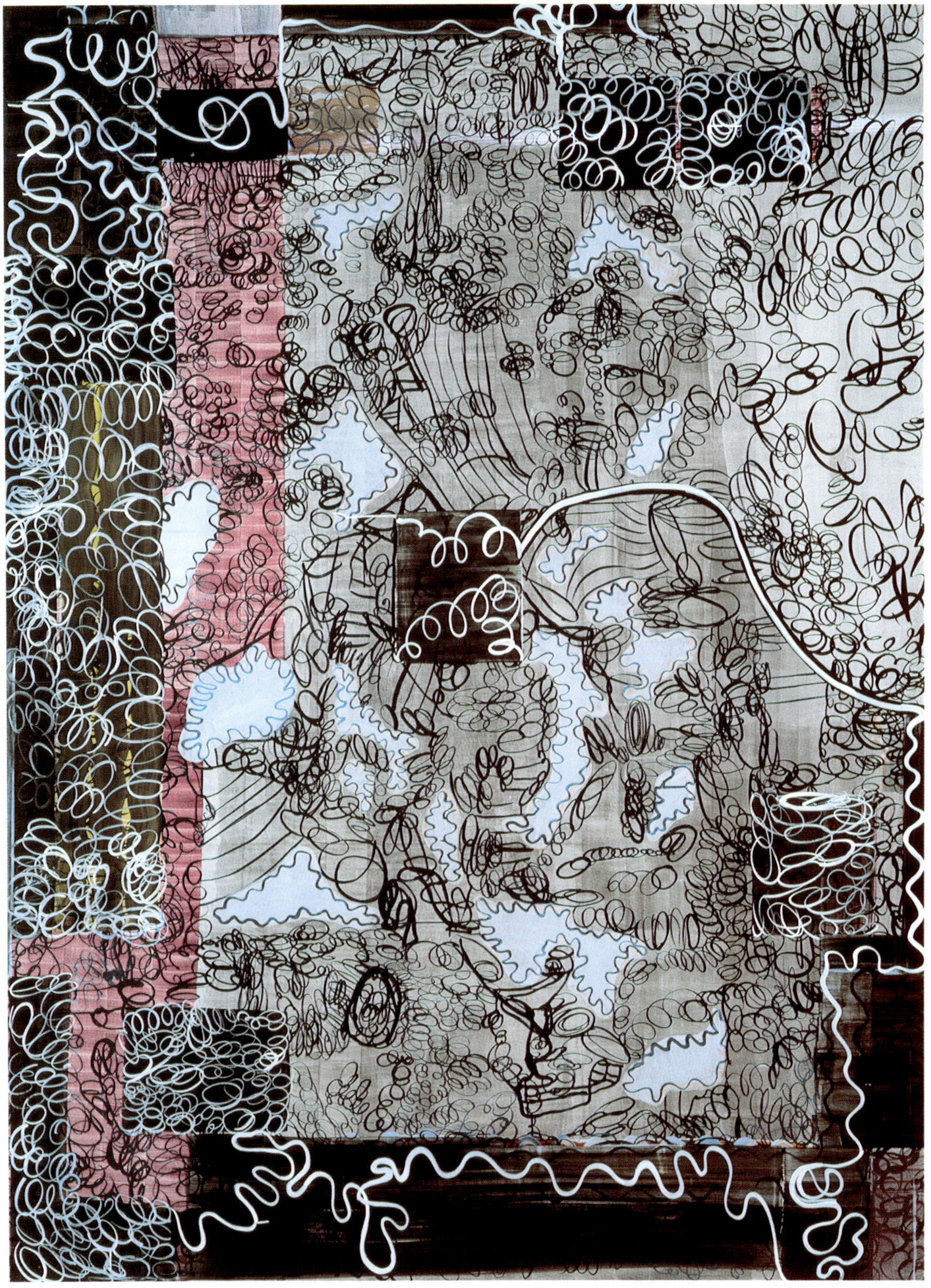

"BILINGUAL"

1998/99

VINYL, DISPERSION UND PIGMENT AUF LEINWAND · 274 X 203 CM

VINYL, EMULSION AND PIGMENT ON CANVAS · 108 X 80 IN.

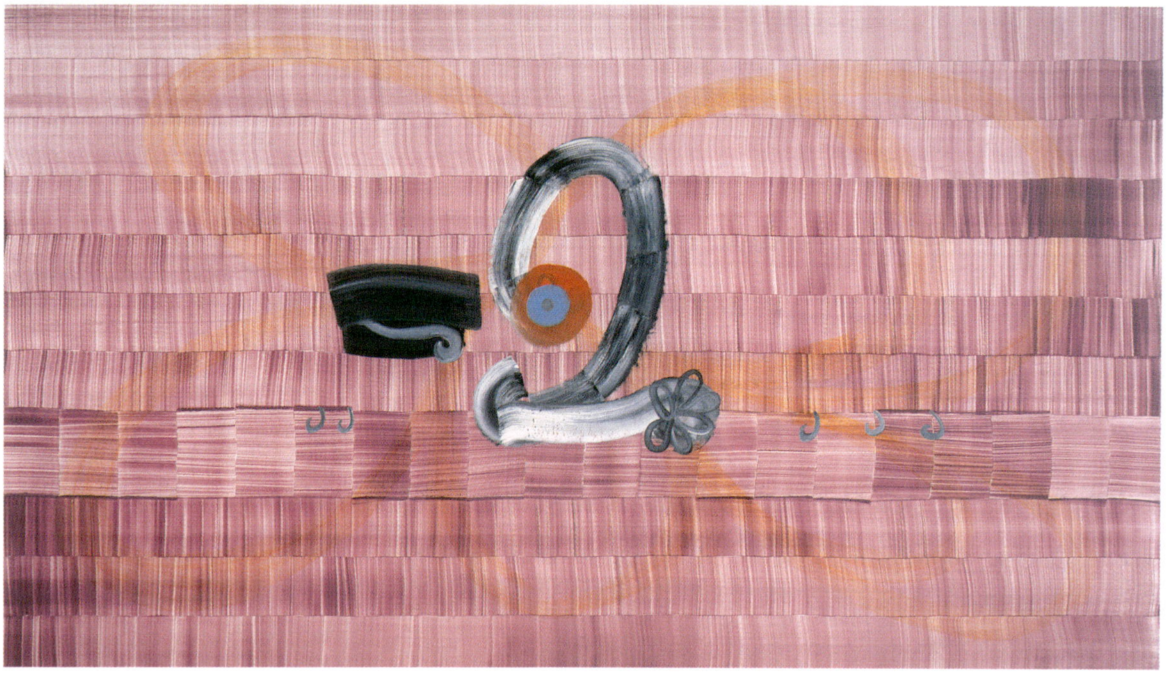

"N° 2 REFLECTING PINBALL"

1999

VINYL, DISPERSION UND PIGMENT AUF LEINWAND · 112 X 198 CM

VINYL, EMULSION AND PIGMENT ON CANVAS · 44 X 78 IN.

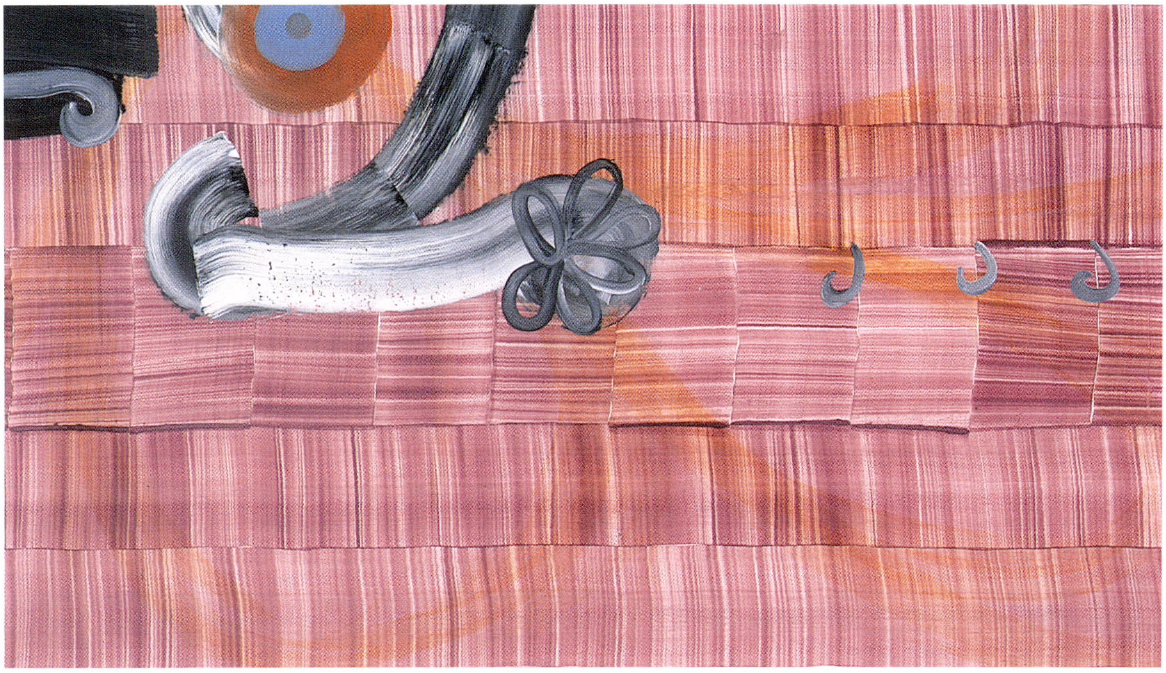

"N° 2 REFLECTING PINBALL" (DETAIL)

1999

VINYL, DISPERSION UND PIGMENT AUF LEINWAND · 112 X 198 CM

VINYL, EMULSION AND PIGMENT ON CANVAS · 44 X 78 IN.

Cover:
© Courtesy Imi Knoebel
"Kosa Belyaka" (Detail)
1998
Acryl auf Aluminium / Acrylic on Aluminium
219,4 x 154,6 x 8,5 cm / 86,4 x 61 x 3,4 in.

Photonachweis/*Photographic Credits*:
John Armleder/Sylvie Fleury: Courtesy ACE Gallery, Los Angeles / Christian Alves de Aranjo
Christian Eckart/Fabian Marcaccio/Jason Martin: Christian Alves de Aranjo
Helmut Federle: Angelika Hausenblas
Mary Heilmann: Tom Warren, courtesy Pat Hearn Gallery, New York
Imi Knoebel: Nic Tenwiggenhorn
David Reed: Dennis Cowley
Gerhard Richter: Courtesy Anthony d´Offay Gallery, London
Günter Umberg: Alistair Overbruck

Text/*Text*: © Christine Buci-Glucksmann
Übersetzungen/*Translations*: Anne Lösch & Charles Penwarden
Gestaltung & Redaktion/*Coordination & Layout*: Günter Salzmann
Druck/*Printed by*: La Linea · Salzburg
Auflage/*Edition*: 1500

A-5020 Salzburg · Mirabellplatz 2 · Tel +43 662 881 393
F-75003 Paris · 7, rue Debelleyme · Tel +33 1 4272 9900

ISBN 3-901935-04-5